# The Christianese Dating Culture

On Courtship, Purity Rings, Prayer-Sex,
and Other Weird Things We Do In Church
by J.S. Park

Citation Information: J.S. Park, *The Christianese Dating Culture* (Florida: The Way Everlasting Ministry, 2014)

Join me in the journey of faith.

Wordpress: http://jsparkblog.com
Facebook: http://facebook.com/pastorjspark
Tumblr: http://jspark3000.tumblr.com
Podcast: http://thewayeverlasting.libsyn.com

# Dedicated

*To my fiancé: I'm writing a book on dating
and you've seen all the ways I've gone wrong.
Yet you have such grace, such fortitude,
in the face of all I've done.*

# Flipping The Table
# of Christianese Contents

# Foreword

# We've Seen Each Other

We've seen each other in line at the movies for tickets to the next rom-com, at the grocery store for a magazine's tips for how to make him swoon, and at the bookstore buying self-help books about love languages, and anything else that will make us better competitors in this battlefield of love.

Dating rituals didn't emerge until about two hundred years ago, and two hundred years later, we're all still trying to figure out when to text back, how to not "lead them on," "how far is too far," and "when to have the DTR," since of course, "to be FBO or not to be FBO—*that* is the question."

All joking and cliché dating jargon aside, romantic relationships and all they entail permeate our thoughts, conversations, future hopes, and present fears. Ultimately, we just don't want to be alone. Isn't that what we're all running from? We want purpose, and how can we find purpose apart from love? Our deepest emotional need is to be seen and affirmed for who we are—told that we're enough, that we matter, and most of all, that we are *wanted.*

Many of us believe that our best shot at finding this is in the face of romance, so we consume and collect all the tactics we can get our hands on. Love is projected like a puzzle, and we've all been set loose in a frenzy searching for all the pieces so we won't be the last to put it together. Even once we might have finished the puzzle, we suspiciously wonder if there's any glue so it won't fall apart.

A fish doesn't know it's wet until it's out of water. What I mean is that it's hard to consider our own experience until we're confronted with something different. It's important that we realize that everyone grew up in a different pond hearing different advice, gathering different philosophies about dating, and developing different habits.

This is what my pond looked like growing up. I grew up going to purity class every year. One session, they presented us with fine china teacups and then held up a styrofoam cup and asked us which one we wanted to be. I wish I would have been able to see through that crooked presentation instead of being bullied into a self-righteous performance-driven understanding of purity. It cornered me into a place of fear, hoping desperately that I'd never mess up.

I wasn't allowed to date until I was 16, yet by the time I was entering high school, a full row on my book shelf fell under the dating category. There was a time I believed that "The Notebook" was emotional porn, that it was promiscuous to be alone in a room with the opposite sex, that saying "I love you" meant I wasn't "guarding my heart," and the fact that I had lost three different purity rings was more likely a scheme of the devil himself than my knack for misplacing things. That metal token never did more than create awkward conversations with strangers in the grocery aisle.

I had one boyfriend in high-school. We dated for two years and never kissed. We didn't want things to "get out of hand." I laugh and roll my eyes at this memory, trying to figure out how I could be so silly and so serious at the same time.

Fast forward to my first semester in college on a couch in a dim room with a guy who wasn't my boyfriend. My first kiss. I was realizing that the rest of the world didn't think kissing was a big deal, and starting to consider crossing over to their side of the court. Even though I had nothing to feel guilty about, I felt like I couldn't tell my friends—the girls who I'd grown up with in the thick humidity of Southern Purity Culture.

I grew up thinking there was only one way to date and it was the only right one. It's true to say that there are unhealthy dating habits, but that people in unhealthy relationships don't really know any different. So, it isn't that every way is okay. [Someone who swallows a whole Oreo without chewing still ate the cookie, but it's obvious that there's a better, safer, more enjoyable way to go about ingesting an Oreo.] We do have a platform of truth to stand on in this discussion, so from there, we can begin a conversation with all of us desiring to establish a healthy, fulfilling, enjoyable philosophy of dating, and that doesn't mean we'll all reach the same conclusion.

The problem is not the purity rings, dating, or anything else for that matter. The problem is our obsession with designating things into black or white when there's a whole sea of grey. With dating, it's important that we all show up with our unique thoughts and opinions, but we can engage a conversation that seeks to rid ourselves of any ideologies or habits that withhold the joy and freedom that Christ's love has purchased for us.

My point is not that you should throw your convictions to the wind. Rather, it's that wherever you fall on the spectrum of dating— whether you're a serial dater, or you've never been on a date—know that we've pulled up a seat just for you. You can take a deep breath and stop looking over your shoulder, fearing who is judging you for either being too uptight or too loose in your approach to dating. I'd like to usher you into a place that is drenched in grace and coated with wisdom as you do yourself a favor and join a conversation that seeks redemption within a realm of reality.

I don't want to point my finger in any specific direction. The long list of misconceptions, self-assigned penance, guilt-induced convictions, and overall uptightness that the church's dating culture has influenced is not our parent's fault, or our youth minister's, or the authors of dating books.

It began with the brokenness that traces back to the Fall when the first humans did exactly what we would have done, by believing that God owed them something more than Himself and that He was withholding something from them. In the same mentality, we chase after security, purpose, and affirmation in people who are chasing the same thing instead of returning to our first love—the one who offers fulfillment and encourages us to imitate this life-giving love in the way we connect with others.

We were made for connection, but when we believe that our relationship status is the only way to fulfillment, we will spiral into an unhealthy paradigm. The purity classes and the promise rings and the dating section of Christian bookstores put a simple, concrete puzzle together throughout my middle school and high-school years. [We are all broken, so if we are going to join the commentary on how truth pertains to relationships, we're going to have to stop drawing attention to each other's debris and acknowledge our own.] And maybe it's our pieces of debris that will allow us to put the pieces together—not to be "solved," but a wholeness to live in as the Lord brings healing, meeting our ultimate needs for purpose, security, and affirmation. And once we find wholeness through our true love, we can be demonstrators of this wholeness—tracing the cracks that remain as testimonials of how we've been reassembled— personalized maps of redemption that tell a story far more compelling than perfection.

This love finds us where we are and promises to carry us, to change us, and to use our lives for His glory, for our satisfaction, and for the benefit of others. When my peer group, my environment, and my way of thinking were all changing, one thing remained—I still believed that truth was relevant. The more life I lived, the more questions I asked, and the more my static and stiff ideologies began to bend and grow and blossom.

From one of the books that sat on the row above my dating collection, an introductory sentence read, "God has spoken and the rest is commentary." That is what these pages hold—commentary.

There is truth, and with the spirit's leading, when we seek to uphold truth in the way we live, this is applied wisdom. My friend J. has quite a story, and it's an account of how truth has given new shape to his life. Here, you will not find a dating manual, but a commentary on truth and how to apply it within the vast topic of romantic relationships.

I think it's worth a shot, because I wish that the middle-school me would have had access to a book like this just as much as I wish the college freshman version of myself would have. [All I ever wanted was someone to look at me and tell me that choosing to not kiss my boyfriend in high-school didn't make me a teacup, and my choice to kiss someone I barely knew in college did not make me a styrofoam cup.]

Maybe you'll reach the last page of this book without a single aspect of your mindset being altered, or maybe you'll find a thoroughly edited version of yourself at the end. There isn't an agenda for either. My only hope is that you'd be willing to shed any pride or apathy you might have and that you'd open yourself to commentary.

— **Lauren Britt** of yesdarlingido.tumblr.com

# Preface
# "I Don't Want To Be *That* Guy"

Sex and relationships can be an absolutely beautiful, wonderful blessing.

But in the Christian subculture of shrill Bible-shaming and shrieking guilt-trips, the one area we've bombed is relationships, which has squeezed many Christian couples into a neurotic, twitchy, anxiety-driven mess.

Some of the things we've heard in church about sex might be the reason why some of us left, or why we think the Bible is outdated, irrelevant, and past its prime.

If we need another book on Christian dating, maybe it's to get a handle on all the other books on Christian dating.

Every piece of Christian advice I've ever heard about relationships tends to boil down to a few simple things.

*"If you're not dating for marriage, you'll ruin your life."*

*"If you've physically crossed the line, it's too late for you."*

*"Sex is gross and disgusting and sinful. So save it for marriage."*

Some of these statements probably began with good intentions. It's right to be cautious whom you date, to guard your own body, to watch out for co-dependency and idolatry. But out of fear, so many well-meaning Christians blew up these ideas into restrictive prisons, in the desperate hope that "You don't want to be like *that* guy." And really, none of that has to do with the God of the Bible or the grace that He offers.

The truth is that many of us are already walking in the consequences of bad decisions we've made. Most of us are already *that* guy. So am I. When one more book or preacher or mentor tells me the consequences to correct me, it's like describing the water that I'm drowning in. It's throwing desert sand for the thirsty. I don't need more guilt-trips. We need wisdom, freedom, and a second chance. It's easy to preach ideals and speak about "standards," but it's harder to roll up our sleeves and get into our tattered trenches.

I want to meet you there, in that honest space. That's where God is.

You see: Jesus loves *that guy* too. He has grace for people like you and me, for those who didn't get it right the first lap around.

I believe that the Christian faith not only has the thoughtfulness to navigate the tricky waters of relationships, but also the grace and healing and restoration for those who have totally messed it up. I believe that Christianity is not only a fountain for the dry and empty, but also a healing salve for those bruised and weary. Whether you're single, divorced, married, on your third marriage, or you're dating for the very first time, I believe the Bible has timeless truth for every condition, every consequence, and every seeking soul.

In these pages, you'll read some observations here about our current Christianese dating culture. You'll read some wisdom to consider for dating. I sincerely invite disagreement about these things, and I would rather we think together to arrive to a better conclusion. Like everyone else, I'm just as likely to "preach further than I really am," and I'll be the first to confess I'm wrestling with all the things written here. You'll also read some real heartbreaking messages I've received over the years. These are real stories, real people, with tough questions. I can't promise to have all the answers, but I hope to point the right direction, towards the *What-Do-I-Do-Now*, and to The One who speaks life into hurting places. And throughout the book, we'll be on a big-picture journey of our church culture, not merely to criticize or complain, but to construct something better from all the ways we've failed.

I want to dismantle some of the lies that we believe about dating, so that we can breathe again.

I want to find what really works, what's really going to shape you into the person God wants you to be for dating, for marriage, for life.

I want to meet you in your heartache, your fear, your future, where loneliness has crept in and you're replaying all the wrong things you did.

I want you to know that the fight for purity is never easy, but it's both possible and worth it.

I want you to know that your mistakes don't say everything about you.

I want you to know that Jesus is the author of second chances, of your faith-story and your love-story, of re-creating you no matter what you've done or who you've become.

Here we find the Greatest Love, before we find love.

Here you will find grace.

—J.S.

# Chapter 1
# Questioning Our Questions About Sex And Dating

## *Speaking Christianese:*
## *A Cycle of Reactionary Backlash, Ad Nauseam*

*"Here's how the Bible starts: with a naked man, singing rapturous love songs over a naked woman in the presence of God. And that's just the start. Go to the book of Proverbs, there's a great passage that says 'A husband needs to be ravished with his wife's breasts.' There's kind of no way around that one. A lot of people ask, 'You're not one of those fundamentalists who takes the Bible literally, are you?' Well sometimes there's an advantage to taking the Bible literally.*

*"… The Bible is filled with bare-faced, exuberant rejoicing in the glory of sexual love. There's no way from the Bible that you can get a negative view of sexual desire."[1]*
— Timothy Keller

When it comes to sex and dating and relationships, most Christian authors and pastors and bloggers are

1) So afraid that their church will have crazy rampant sexy time that they set these impossible nun-like standards, and

2) Telling us How-To Pragmatic Formulas we try for a while until we totally face-plant.

Both of these false foundations have led to the Christianese Dating Culture.

Let's tackle the first one, about backlash.

---

[1] Timothy Keller's sermon "Lust and Love," May 6, 2012

I understand the need to throw a morality around sex within the church, because churches feel the pressure to run against lazy ideas perpetuated in Hollywood rom-coms. And certainly there are tons of dysfunctional views on sex out there that have indoctrinated their tendrils into our impressionable minds. We don't always realize how many lies we've actually bought into.

Yet we've run so violently the other way that we've demonized sexuality into a monster, which represses all our healthy sexual desires and feeds a toxic culture of silence and fear.

While wisdom is necessary, repression is *never* a good thing. Empirical studies about *"reactance theory"* will tell you that the more you limit the freedom of a particular choice, the more such resistance will both tempt us into the forbidden fruit and imprison us with an indecisive confusion.[2] In other words, when we're overly threatened *not* to do something, we'll either go for it with more force or we'll be paralyzed on how to move forward.

The irony here is that the church is yelling so obnoxiously against Hollywood-type romance that we're alienating those who have already fallen for Hollywood-type romance. We're championing rules that most people have already broken, so most churchgoers who hear about sex and dating in the church walk away feeling hopeless, helpless, or harangued. Some of us live in perpetual guilt over feeling "impure" or we feel contempt against the close-minded moralism of the pulpit.

In the area of sex: the church is either churning out prodigals or we're making the marriage bed a nightmare. We've been good at *running away* from something but not *toward* anything else. Many of us

---

[2] Check out studies by Brehm & Brehm 1981, Aronson & Carlsmith 1963, and Legault, Gutsell, & Inzlicht 2011. The middle experiment is the famous "Forbidden Toys," in which preschoolers who were threatened not to play with a certain toy found it more desirable. The latter experiment demonstrates an "Ironic Effect of Anti-Prejudice," in which those told to reduce their prejudice were generally likely to be even more racist later on.

are saying, "Don't be like those other guys," so we jump to the other extreme.

Any preacher or book or conference that's simply responding to someone else's response is creating a circular platform, where none of the sermonizing is actually speaking to *real people.*

With sex and dating and relationships — even with faith and life and the daily grind — the church is mostly telling you what *not* to do. We're fighting invisible phantoms and made-up enemies.

Please know that I absolutely *love* the church, and I don't want to be one more guy who badmouths her. I just know we could do better because I believe we're serving the Author of Truth, and He is way more balanced than our lopsided overreaction to one of God's greatest gifts.

Let's take a look at the church for a moment. In the 1990s, there was the Seeker-Sensitive Movement where the word "seeker" replaced sinner. They offered a "mainstream service" minus the wrath of God and the blood-of-the-lamb, so you could finally bring your atheist neighbor to church. The Reformed Calvinists pushed back and declared a return to traditionalism and "right doctrine." Soon the Mystics and the Emergent (Hipster) Church retorted by communing with God through rivers and mountains and fair trade coffee. Then there was a fist-pump for social justice and a nose-up at mega-churches, but very little talk of purity or holiness or doctrine.

We see this pattern everywhere. We see it in Protestantism versus Catholicism. There are entire ministries born from previous hurts in another church to show up "those other Christians." You could be part of one. Sometimes when I hear a sermon, I sense the preacher is attacking something "worldly" or calling out some "sin" in his church or responding to a pastor across the street. It's the preacher's personal catharsis. I've done this too. The sad part is, no one in the congregation cares about this — with the sole exception of the

Christianese choir. I've almost never heard a clear-headed sermon on sex and dating that begins from the wisdom and grace of Christ. It often begins by bashing a straw-man with other straw-men.

On and on, the **Cycle of Reactionary Backlash** goes, a circus carousel of revolving theologies and ministries and philosophies. These are layers upon layers of damage and dissension that have buried the foundation.

I'm probably defeating my own point here by pointing fingers and responding to responses, but I'm grieving in my heart for unity. I truly believe we can learn from each other if we first recognize that none of us have the monopoly on all there is to say about faith and life.

You can probably trace *every single movement in history* as a reaction to a previous movement or mode of thought.

So why is all this important?

Because, my dear friend: *We're all products of our time, living in a whirlwind of someone else's predominant interpretation of how things ought to be.*

Many of these pendulum swings were necessary rebuilding.

But a few, out of deep mistrust, set their walls too high and their fists too tight.

I know at this point it sounds easier to say, "Let's just throw out every idea about dating and we can figure it out ourselves. Forget Hollywood and religion and everything in between: I got this."

But the problem there, of course, is that this is *just another reaction.* It's still being pushed around between ideologies.

What God really wants is not for us to perpetuate a back-and-forth ricochet of ideas, but to live a life that's initiated from life. It's to originate life from The One who created it. Just as God is the Creator, who made everything *ex nihilo,* out of nothing, God is also a continually creating God. He shaped a formless chaotic mass into order, and He's still doing this. We have that same spark in us, to create. Otherwise, we build movements out of opposition, which only breed smug self-righteousness. If we do this long enough, the values we instill into our new culture will be based in bitterness and arrogance. These are unstable poisonous foundations that will inevitably collapse.

We can start up movements that are *not reactions, but initiative actions.*

Our words can be *not talking back, but talking forward.*

We can be original instead of derivative.

We don't have to be motivated solely by the pain we feel —

because even though it can work for a while, healing cannot come by deconstruction.

**Healing only comes by re-creation, by introducing something new into the world.**

We each have this powerful ability to weaponize our words or to breathe life with them.

Our hands can build bridges toward oblivion or toward each other.

I hope for bridges that bring us closer.

All this really is a small glimpse of what Jesus did for us on the cross.

He was starting from scratch, to absorb our cycle of hurt, and to re-write the story.

He began the birth of the *something new*, wholly above our human nature, a place of rest.

Our faith and family and love-life can finally be free to breathe.

I hope you see how important this is for our sexual theology. Neither sexual repression nor sexual leniency can work for us. A healthy view of sexuality requires a bold, brazen, unabashed honesty about our desires, emotions, insecurities, and physicality, while at the same time viewing sexuality as one of the most sacred, vulnerable, sensitive areas of the human heart.

Without such a willingness for open conversation in the church, we're left in the back-and-forth whiplash of angry repressed preachers or cool casual hipsters, and everyone's just reacting to everyone else. I want to get to the very *core* of relational truth, about how we can approach this from God's point of view, without the mucky stains of my passive-aggressive commentary. I want to strip the layers of what the church has been telling me, and get back to the God who made me.

### *Speaking Christianese Fluently: Our Modern Obsession With Flexing Technique*

The second cause of the Christianese dating culture is a lot more insidious and subtle. It's partially a symptom of the Western mentality of productivity and pragmatism and our growing obsession with efficiency.

I do believe we need good advice for what's ahead.

We need safe-guards and behavioral roadmaps to be our true selves.

But any time a Christian enters into a checklist of Good Habits and Warning Signs and Ten-Ways-To-Be-Hot-And-Holy, they're swamped by a rule-based morality that can only beat you up into resentful submission or prideful perfectionism.

Our Christianese culture is armed to the teeth with more practical methodology than ever. But we're only re-doing the paint, over and over, without checking the engine or destination.

We scramble for the Secret Sauce on sex and dating, yet I want to ask:

*Why? What's the purpose? Where is this going?*

I'm reminded of a sermon by Matt Chandler:

*"It seems like everything's built on pragmatism. A plus B equals C. If you want C, do A, do B, you'll get C. Here's what 'we do.' It's going well there, let me do what they do. ... I'm not saying planning is wrong. But where is that man whose heart is aflame for God, that God is enough?"* [3]

I've said before that *advice without Christ is living without life.*

Please know that I believe rules are good. The Law of God is for our benefit. We do need discipline and methods. I love sermons with practical application and the Five Things You Must Do. Yet I believe there is no one more unhappy and empty than a person built on scaffolding. Self-regulation is eventually exhausting and dreary. Only a person "whose heart is aflame for God" is fulfilled enough to follow through.

If we don't first begin from a place of God's very own purpose in why we pursue things, then we're only following boundaries for the sake of boundaries. This kills any passion of the pursuit itself. It's like learning dance moves to look good on the dance floor, but never knowing the *soul* and *art* of dance for its own essence. We too easily spiral into a secret inward competition of head-knowledge and technical savvy to look like a good spouse — instead of becoming one. Love-Languages and Love-Dares might save your marriage, but ultimately they're just *doing Christian things around God instead of Christ-centered life* **with** *Him.*

I had really bought into the modern Christianese idea of dating because it appeals to the legalistic Pharisee in all of us. And most Christianese dating advice is quite terrible, so I wasn't even a good Pharisee. It's not all bad, but it often results in a panicked paranoia about the opposite sex that leads to unhealthy self-slavery.

You see, I can do one of two things for you as a pastor, as a Christian, as your friend. I can beat you up with rules and religion —

---

[3] Matt Chandler, "Preaching The Gospel To The De-Churched," the Advance Conference, June 15th 2009. https://www.youtube.com/watch?v=d4jMFOJTglk

"Do more, try harder!" — and I can make you conform your behavior. Like that guy who makes you jump during worship. It would be an external apparatus working on your outside, but *it would never become a part of you.* You'll get short-term change, but Monday through Saturday when the fear is gone, the change won't last.

Or the second thing I can do is, I can tell you about the **grace of God** — where God loves you no matter what, without conditions, even counter-conditionally, through the depth of our very worst, at the cost of His very Son. So then our actions would spring out of gratitude for what He has done for us and for who He is. That comes not just from rules and religion, though those are important, but from a real, pulsing, thriving relationship with the living God. That's the only pure sustainable motivation. Grace can take a lot longer than guilt-trips, but in the long-term, *grace is the only power that can internalize to change your heart.*

The point can't be about the tactics or methods or techniques, but always asking **what's the main purpose** and **where is this taking me.** The point of all these methods is not to have good methods, but to re-focus back on the journey itself, continually empowered by God's re-shaping love.

*Only when we're free from merely following the rules can we see the good that the rules point to.* And I believe that the God of the Bible not only has a good law for us to follow, but His Law will bring us back to the heart who made us.

## *The Great Theologians, Apostle Paul and Taylor Swift*

*"This world is a great sculptor's shop. We are the statues and there's a rumor going around the shop that some of us are someday going to come to life."* [4]
— C.S. Lewis     *wow i love this*

Before we dissect the bizarre subculture of Christianese dating, I want to back way up.

Before any talk about dating, I want to talk about **identity**.

I know that's a Christianese word used for sermons and scholars, and not used much elsewhere. But *identity* is probably the most important thing we could ever talk about, mostly because we don't talk about it.

There's a passage from 2 Timothy that churchgoers love to amen all day long. Me included. It's the equivalent of throwing a baseball bat at a mosquito.

**V.22** — *Flee the evil desires of youth, and pursue righteousness, faith, love and peace, along with those who call on the Lord out of a pure heart.*

I've heard sermons built on this one verse, and they were very good sermons.

But *half a picture of the correct truth is an incorrect picture of the whole truth.*

This verse has a few verses before it that paint a much broader portrait of not just lust, but our entire lives. Here's the context.

---

[4] C.S. Lewis, *Mere Christianity* (New York: HarperCollins, 1952, 1980), p. 103

**V.20-21** — *In a large house there are articles not only of gold and silver, but also of wood and clay; some are for noble purposes and some for ignoble. If a man cleanses himself from the latter, he will be an instrument for noble purposes, made holy, useful to the Master and prepared to do any good work.*

So Apostle Paul, the author of this passage, first tackles the much larger question of *who we are*. He asks the identity question before the dating question. Paul says that in God's house, we are each like finely crafted instruments made of gold or silver or wood or clay, and that each of us have a purpose for the Master, prepared to do any good work. Before Paul talks about anything else, he talks about **what we're really about.**

In other words, while the church culture has mostly hammered away at the area of sex with a myopic view of purity, Paul has a much higher view of sex by prioritizing our spirituality.

It sounds lofty, so I'll put this backwards to make it easier.

*If your struggle with lust today was completely over:*

*What else would you be doing instead?*

*What if your entire struggle with sin was done? What now?*

*What if all your questions about dating were completely answered? What then?*

When someone tells me about their romantic curiosity or their constant crushes or their out-of-control urges, I think of the great theologian Taylor Swift.[5]

*"'Cause when you're fifteen and somebody tells you they love you*

*You're gonna believe them*

*And when you're fifteen / Feeling like there's nothing to figure out*

*Well count to ten, take it in*

*This is life before you know who you're gonna be / Fifteen"*

---

[5] I was inspired by this illustration from Andy Stanley in his sermon series, "Love, Sex, & Dating." All the credit on this one goes to him, though I'm taking it in a different direction.

When you feel that first stab of impulse towards a romantic interest, that first time is always overwhelming and dramatic, because it's the first time. It'll throw you off. The first crush, first heartbreak, and first internal back-flip of hormones is always a sweeping rush, and no one could blame you for that. The verse about "Flee the evil desires of youth" gets buried under the flare of this new fire.

But when Paul is writing all the stuff about gold and clay, he's saying —

*Let's ask some questions first.*

*Who are you? What is your primary objective? What are you about?*

*Who am I? What is my primary objective? What am I about?*

Or: *Don't let those emotions get you all hot and bothered yet.*

When the feelings of lust or romance come, whether legitimate or not, and they will, we can back up and ask some important questions. We can pause to *think* before we react. In the midst of seemingly overpowering butterflies, we can sit down to be thoughtful over our motives and momentum.

I can't simply tell you how to do relationships.

I want us to talk about why.

We can ask even more specifically:

*Why do I want to be in a relationship? Why this person?*

*Where did I learn my idea of relationships from? Am I taking my cue from culture?*

*Where are these feelings coming from? Are they based in a mature understanding of relationships or a derivative pseudo-romance from some movies I watched?*

*What will happen if I follow through with this?*

*Am I even ready for anything like this?*

*What are my motives? Am I longing for this because I'm afraid of being alone? Because I dislike being single? Or because this person is cute in the face?*

This isn't to say that we're totally dismissing romantic feelings as puppy-love or misguided immaturity. Our desires are *not* wrong. It's that our desires have a priority. **God wants us to be a people who are so completely satisfied in Him that we can rightly handle the things of the earth.**

C.S. Lewis put it best here:

*"The longings which arise in us when we first fall in love, or first think of some foreign country, or first take up some subject that excites us, are longings which no marriage, no travel, no learning, can really satisfy. I am not now speaking of what would be ordinarily called unsuccessful marriages, or holidays, or learned careers. I am speaking of the best possible ones. There was something we grasped at, in that first moment of longing, which just fades away in the reality.*

*"... Probably earthly pleasures were never meant to satisfy it, but only to arouse it, to suggest the real thing. If that is so, I must take care, on the one hand, never to despise, or be unthankful for, these earthly blessings, and on the other, never to mistake them for the something else of which they are only a kind of copy, or echo, or mirage. I must keep alive in myself the desire for my true country, which I shall not find till after death; I must never let it get snowed under or turned aside; I must make it the main object of life to press on to that other country and to help others to do the same."[6]*

You see: We're each created, made, and saved by Christ for Christ. In Jesus, you have a **love** that will never forsake you, a **mission** bigger than yourself, and a final **home** at the end. If you don't believe this today or you're re-entering the church with caution, that's very much okay. My heart is for you to know the one who made your heart for the best relationship possible. Romance is wonderful, but it's one of the many things that actually points to the Creator of everything, just as a strand of sunlight points back to the author of the sun. The heat of romantic emotion is a window into the Eternal Romance that you were made for.

---

[6] C.S. Lewis, *Mere Christianity* (New York: HarperCollins, 1952, 1980), p. 135-137

**Before thinking about relationships, we're designed to have relational intimacy with God.** It's not merely that Adam and Eve "disobeyed" God in the Garden, but they were disconnected from Him too. They severed their true source of love and goodness and glory. Our significance and validation comes from Him. Without this, we'll merely pursue our latest loudest feelings to accumulate more feelings, which is a bottomless perpetuity that will crush others and crush ourselves. You know what I mean. If you finally land that relationship you so badly wanted, your initial illusions always go out the window, and suddenly this person isn't fulfilling you like you'd hoped. It hurts that person and hurts you, too.

We often demand of people what only God can give us — encouragement, affirmation, strength, motivation — and we end up wringing others dry. It's okay to expect some things from people, so long as you know they're just human beings who thirst like you. They need an Infinite Well as much as you do. If you drink deeply of Him first, you'll be less controlled (and controlling) by your expectations, and you'll actually seek others not to squeeze from them but to encourage them by your overflow.

We must first know ourselves before we get to know anyone else, and **our one irrevocable identity is found in Him.**

As Francis Chan says in his book about marriage:
*"When two people are right with Him, they will be right with each other ... Most marriage problems are not really marriage problems. They are God problems. They can be traced back to one or both people having a poor relationship with God or a faulty understanding of Him. An accurate picture of God is vital to a healthy marriage. It's vital to everything."*[7]

When you can let go of the idols of relationships, wealth, intellect, success, beauty, and career, you can actually enjoy them for what they are. You don't expect salvation or redemption from them.

---

[7] Francis & Lisa Chan, *You and Me Forever* (California: Claire Love, 2014) p. 20-21

You don't crush them with expectations nor do you demand them to serve your every whim. You instead see them as gifts, as privileges, as an honor to respect and to cherish. Treat the earthly as divine and you will lose both; treat the divine as your treasure and the earth will be just as beautiful.

It's only out of the wellspring of God's infinite love for you that we can begin to live and love without expecting fulfillment from people and things. And when I'm engaged with the mission for which God has specifically tailored for me, then I'm able to rightly estimate everything else in my life. Not perfectly, but finally, with a path set before us.

Let's dig a little deeper.

## *Tsunamis, Shotguns, and Naked Windows*

One of my favorite tropes in movies is when two people are arguing, and suddenly outside the window, there's a large danger approaching. In a moment, their petty argument stops because of the impending doom outside.

Susie and Johnny are yelling at each other for some asinine reason, and then they notice a giant tsunami about to flatten their house.

Susie was just yelling, "It's not what you said, it's how you said it!" Johnny was just yelling, "You always do this! And you never do that!"

But they see the hundred foot tidal wave through the window, and both stop mid-sentence. Then Susie says, *"I've always loved you, Johnny."* And they make up seconds before the tsunami gets them.

In the face of a much bigger force, we always find what's most important. But more than that, *the larger force always displaces the smaller one.*

When someone tells me it's impossible to beat lust, I often bring up the idea of a *"larger force displacing a smaller force."* Usually they just blink at me and make the face that says "All you pastors talk like that."

Here's the idea.[8] If you're getting hot and heavy with your girlfriend and you supposedly get past some point of "no return," and then her five-star military father barges in with a Remington double-barrel shotgun, you'll magically stop yourself. You're not going to say to her father, "I'm past the point of no return, sir." You're either on your knees begging for forgiveness or you're jumping out the window butt-naked. It's because the larger force of the military dad and his shotgun outweighed the smaller force of your loins.

Not only do we need an expulsive power to push out the chokehold of destructive patterns, but there's an *Ultimate Power* who we're actually designed to live for. It's by His very nature that all other things are downsized to their proper volume. And He is bigger than the tsunami, bigger than the shotgun, bigger than our lust and longing. He's not merely a tool to beat our daily problems, but the *Answer* to every problem there ever was, and the *Author* of all we will ever do and become.

**The only way to fight sin is to *choose something bigger instead*.** That sounds too simple, but for every couple who is fighting to keep physical boundaries, I find out that this is *all* they're doing. They're fighting sin to fight sin and it never works.

Have you ever noticed Galatians 5:16?

*"So I say, walk by the Spirit, and you will not gratify the desires of your flesh."*

In other words: *Choose the things of God, and you will have no room to choose anything else.*

---

[8] I'd like to thank Pastor J.D. Greear for this one, who tells it much better than I do.

Here's what I've learned about choosing the things of God and partaking in His mission.

I've noticed that after I disciple a young kid and see his eyes light up from the truth of the Bible, I can't go back to how I was. It's too good to give up. After I serve food at the homeless ministry, after I volunteer at a retreat, after I go on a mission trip, after I serve at an orphanage or a prison or the projects — the attraction of sin loses its grip on me.

Because the things of God are so much brighter and bigger and deeper than the things of this world. This is what Thomas Chalmers called *the Expulsive Power of a New Affection.*

Ever notice that after the gym, you're too tired to fight anyone? Ever notice that after a healthy meal, you're much less willing to eat a bag of Cheetos? And whether you "feel like" going to the gym or eating healthy, you can choose to do them anyway, because not only is the alternative bad for you, but it makes the alternative *less attractive.*

Sometimes people wait to "feel right with God" to go serve Him. You don't have to wait. You don't have to be qualified or clean or deserving to serve. **Your choices change your heart just as much as your heart changes your choices.** What you do comes out of who you are, but who you are also comes out of what you do.

Certainly there are hypocrites who lead double lives. But at some point, the cognitive dissonance becomes too much to bear, and they either settle into their faith or walk away. I pray you settle in for good.

## *Ripping The Roof Off The Drama*

Here's the other thing. In the Tsunami-Scenario, we also learn an inverse truth — that when there's nothing bigger than ourselves, our focus *must* go somewhere, and it's often towards lesser things. Ecclesiastes 3:11 tells us that *"God has set eternity in the heart of man,"* meaning that we're made to be filled with no less than the eternal glory of God. Since the eternity inside us is always there, we're not just made to fill it, but constantly filling on something. Anything less than Christ will have us scrambling for self-made glory, which is always the cheapest kind, so we begin to use romance and money and image in illegitimate ways that are foreign to how we're designed.

I have a cynical theory that the reason most people feel extremely insecure or inordinately bitter is because they have nothing else to focus on. Small innocuous comments are blown up in our heads because we have too much idleness to read into them. Of course, this is highly critical of me, and it doesn't mean that our feelings of discouragement are wrong. Yet to linger on them, live by them, and fester in the comfortable familiarity of our negative thoughts is a rehearsed skill. When we're not within the wonderful drama of God's narrative, we tend to build our own sadder drama.

**When each of us get on the God-given adventure that He has for us, we're able to invite others into the ride that we're already on.** There's something bigger at stake, a horizon to keep in view, a task empowered by The One who knows us best. Otherwise, I would only be inviting a person to myself, and people are not made to endure the unbearable weight of eternity from each other's hearts.

This is why in the middle of Paul's passage on marriage in 1 Corinthians 7, he makes an enigmatic statement that looks like a subject change. But it's not; it's the natural resolution to his train of thought. Paul says in verses 29-31,

*What I mean, brothers, is that the time is short. From now on those who have wives should live as if they had none; those who mourn, as if they did not; those who are happy, as if they were not; those who buy something, as if it were not theirs to keep; those who use the things of the world, as if not engrossed in them. For this world in its present form is passing away.*

Paul is reminding us that we live in the shadow of an overarching story that rose forth from a tomb and we're part of the healing of a shattered world. Everything on earth, while worth enjoying, is going to fade just as much as every stick of furniture in your room. We live within entropy and the unwinding of time; yet God is the only one outside of this, and He controls it all.

My atheist friend used to tell me, "If you make a relationship about the relationship, you'll kill the whole thing. You need something bigger to bring her along." He was right. He was talking about building a business or a name or a life; I'm talking about the Only Name who ever matters, who's in the business of bringing the dead to life. I'm sorry if that was Christianese, but really: the most exciting thing I can do for my own loved ones is to bring them along for the **truest quest** there is, for that fantastic adventure in following Christ. I can't invite them to *me*. I can't die for their sins. I can't set them free. I'm not even qualified to be the boss of myself. I serve The One who is.

Of course drama still happens; conflict is inevitable; we'll still get caught up sometimes. Yet even the conflict has a direction, a current of grace to bring us back, a live wire of power to guide us forward.

I used to live in this apartment complex where I would sit out by the swimming pool to use the wi-fi for my laptop, because I was trying to be a monk without internet at my place (I was too cheap). Across from the pool, there was a couple who would argue all the time with the windows open. A few months in, the girlfriend found her boyfriend cheating with another woman, and all three of them were thrashing and screaming and crying and throwing picture frames. A neighbor stuck his head out the door and told them to shut up, with some extra salty words. The couple yelled back at the neighbor. A few dogs joined in the fight too.

During the middle of their argument, I began to giggle. Really. I tried to contain myself but I couldn't stop giggling. I put my hand over my mouth but then the laughter snorted out of my nostrils and this high-pitched noise came up from the back of my throat through my fingers. My sides were busting open and I got woozy from trying to hold it in so hard. Tears shot down my face. The three people stopped arguing for a second because they heard me laughing. I closed my laptop and ran out of there.

I found the entire situation downright hilarious. I know it was really awful and judgmental of me and I don't mean to say I'm better than them; in fact, I'm the same. I've been in plenty of terrible situations of my own making too. Of course God always has grace for each of us. But it was like that moment when you watch a reality show and you cringe at the shrill spoiled depravity of it all, and suddenly you realize how ridiculous we can become when we're wrapped up in things beneath us.

Halfway back to my own apartment, it wasn't funny anymore. I grew angry and grieved. I was angry at myself. I pictured God ripping the roof off their building and looking down at those three people, His glorious infinite presence towering over the swimming pool, making eye contact and not saying a word. I imagined every tenant in that building bowing down or bursting into flames or just wailing in horror at their own drama. I imagined God ripping the roof off *my* heart, exposing all the wrong attachments and ugly emotions and how often I had strayed from His calling. I imagined the searing love of God, how undeserving I would feel yet so wonderfully safe in His gracious embrace.

If I would've asked the fighting couple about their problems, they probably would've said, "I got some issues with my love-life." Which

The Christianese Dating Culture · 24

is true. But not many of us talk about the elusive word *identity*. That's where it starts. When we're no longer looking up, we're more likely to get sucked into petty trivial things. I know that no one wants that, but it happens by such imperceptible degrees, declining into a shadow kind of life stuck in self-centered drama. I was there, too.

I began to ask myself:

*If I really knew that God is who He says is and did what He said He did —*
*What would I do then?*
*How would I use the gifts and abilities and treasures and strengths that God has bestowed on this one life?*

I believe when we know God is who God is, it would be both absolutely terrifying and overwhelmingly awesome. It would knock us out of our selfish orbits and into the True Story of the world. We wouldn't be the same. We might even be able to stop in the middle of our drama and laugh at ourselves.

## Never, Ever, Ever Too Late

I know the truth is that we've all gotten this wrong somewhere. Many of us have failed to ask the hard questions and we've fallen for lesser things. We've all been that arguing couple in the apartment, and worse. I'm including myself in there. Maybe all this talk about "purpose" and "mission" sounds nice and idealistic to you, but you feel that it's for someone else.

When we hear sermons about sex and dating, a piercing guilt sets in —

*It's too late for me, because I've already messed it up.*

In a Christianese church culture, there's no room for sinners like you and me. You're either in or you're out. You got it or you don't. It's one-shot or it's over.

A sermon on sex or even a book like this can make you feel you lost out on something, like you're somehow beyond His reach. We get locked into a cycle of compensating for our wrongs. The Christianese way is to run, jump, and kick our way through faith.

The truth is that no matter where we are in our "identity" or "purity" or "maturity," *God is going to work with you on this.* This is who He is. God cannot help it. He loves His children, and even those like you and me. **Nothing you do could ever change God's heart towards you, and it's His unchanging heart that changes you.**

We learn in Romans 7 and 1 John 3 that we're in a gap between *who we want to be* and *where we really are.* I do believe we want to pursue the greater story, yet we live in that gray-space struggle where our *heart* and *body* are at crossfire. And this is exactly where God enters. This is where the Christian faith tells us about the God who was not an abstract ideal, but one who stepped into the dirt of the earth as one of us, to call us back to His greatness, and showed such solidarity with us through temptation, weariness, persecution, and abandonment. Jesus so profoundly understands what you're going through more than you could know. He *knows.*

As much as I've been mad at myself for getting so caught up in inconsequential things, I had to remember that God wasn't mad. He knew we would turn against Him and against each other. He sent Jesus for this very reason, to die for all the ways we've wandered, to beckon us home, to be restored and renewed by His breaking of death, to reinstate us back to the men and women He knows we can be.

God extends such grace, always.

It is never, ever, ever too late to return to His royalty, as rightful co-heirs of Christ.

When guilt threatens to overwhelm you, remember who you are: you're a child of God,
forgiven and free,

restored by the work of Jesus on the cross,
resurrected to new life by his victory over death,
and you have the Holy Spirit living inside you
that is not a spirit of fear or timidity,
but of love, power, and self-control.

We don't live in a locked-down house of laws — we live within the free grace of an awesome loving dad who wants us, who loves us, and who *likes* us.

I'll follow that sort of God all the way to the end.

## Let's Have A Conversation

If we were to sit down together over coffee and you asked me advice about dating —

I would ask you questions about your questions about dating.

I would want us to take a huge step back from all the ideas we've heard about courtship and Christianese techniques and practical how-to, and examine the *why*. Examine the *who*.

I would ask about identity. Again, I know that's a cheesy word, but I would ask:

*What is the essential? What is non-essential?*

*What is the qualitative weight of our lives? What's the substance? What's the "telos"?*

*What are you really about?*

**Who** *are you about?*

These are heavy questions, I know.

It's not that we need to figure this out in a day. We don't need to become *everything we need to be* before we think about relationships. The identity stuff is hard work. It takes a day at a time, just like everything else. None of this is easy.

But **when I know who I am,**

when I continue the discovery of The One who made me,

when I'm connected to the purpose and presence and power of True Life,

I can begin to handle everything else. I can discern the *how* and the *what-now*. We can re-purpose ourselves for every sticky, scary, difficult area of this journey together.

Not perfectly, but passionately, by His grace.


Over coffee, I would pray for you. Can you pray for me too? Because we all need prayer on this.

This is so much bigger than highlighting a book on dating.

This is not some fixed formula that will solve your singleness or dating woes by Friday.

This is not "Ten Ways To Baptize Your Marriage."

Of course, the books and formulas and sermons might help.

[*But we need the power of God to become who God has called us to be.*]

So much more is at stake.

This is about the God-sized call on your life.


*For we are God's workmanship, created in Christ Jesus to do good works, which God prepared in advance for us to do.*

— Ephesians 2:10


*[Be] confident of this, that he who began a good work in you will carry it unto completion until the day of Christ Jesus.*

— Philippians 1:6


*But seek first his kingdom and his righteousness, and all these things will be given to you as well. Therefore do not worry about tomorrow, for tomorrow will worry about itself. Each day has enough trouble of its own.*

— Matthew 6:33-34

# Chapter 2
# About Joshua Harris and Good Ideas Gone Wild

In 1997, a book popped up in the Christianese world called *I Kissed Dating Goodbye,* written by a twenty-one year old Joshua Harris. It has since sold over a million copies. Phrases like "courtship," "purposeful singleness," and "principled romance" entered the vocabulary of the pulpit. Preachers and parents latched into this frenzy and rehearsed the mantra, *Dating is wrong and it's only for marriage — or else.*

I've known pastors who name-drop Joshua Harris in every sermon about relationships, either holding him up as the poster boy guru for godly dating, or as the devil who crept into your bed and desecrated your marriage.

I want to tell you up front that I believe Pastor Josh is a fellow brother in Christ, and though I never met him, I love him dearly, and he couldn't have anticipated the force his book would become.

One particular scenario in Josh Harris's book became nightmare fuel for every 1990s church kid.

> *But as the minister began to lead Anna and David through their vows, the unthinkable happened. A girl stood up in the middle of the congregation, walked quietly to the altar, and took David's other hand … Soon, a chain of six girls stood by him as he repeated his vows to Anna.*
>
> *Anna felt her lip begin to quiver as tears welled up in her eyes. "Is this some kind of joke?" she whispered to David.*
>
> *"I'm…I'm sorry, Anna," he said, staring at the floor.*
>
> *"Who are these girls, David? What is going on?" she gasped.*

*"They're girls from my past," he answered sadly. "Anna, they don't mean anything to me now...but I've given part of my heart to each of them."*

*"I thought your heart was mine," she said.*

*"It is, it is," he pleaded. "Everything that's left is yours." A tear rolled down Anna's cheek. Then she woke up.[9]*

Churches built on the idea of "Spiritual Virginity" and "Emotional Purity," where you could irrevocably give away *pieces of your heart* to every person you've dated before you're married. Praying together meant you were having "spiritual prayer-sex." And premature dating would lead to "soul-ties," which means you were anchored to an ex-boyfriend or girlfriend, *forever*. Church leaders would scold the slightest inappropriate gestures in their youth groups, doing a lot of the pulling-aside-for-serious-rebuking, making sure no one had "the appearance of evil."

One blogger said about the teaching on courtship:

**"They cause pride.** *Pride because suddenly you are better than everyone else. Because you have never had a crush on a guy. You have kept your heart for your spouse. You didn't say 'I love you 'til your wedding day. Pride in human accomplishment. Pride because you are so much more spiritual than that poor girl over there who is crying because her boyfriend broke up with her. Because your heart is whole and she just gave a piece of hers to a guy she isn't married to. Pride because you did it right, she did not. You have more to give your future husband than she does. She is damaged goods, you are the real prize."[10]*

Some of the more harsh reviews on Amazon also say:

---

[9] Joshua Harris, *I Kissed Dating Goodbye* (Colorado: Multnomah, 1997) p. 13-14
[10] Darcy from Recovering Grace,
http://www.recoveringgrace.org/2011/07/emotionalpurity/

"This book has basically ruined my life ... This is basically a childish, immature kind of book only meant for youths ... I believe that each person's experience is entirely different than that of the author itself. What about some individuals who have been raped or molested?"

"I'm not just mad at him, but at the Christian culture that fertilized his misguided ideas, and catalyzed their growth into an ivy that has grown over the culture of the Christian single, choking out light and hope for untold numbers of broken hearts."

"If you read Harris' next book, he didn't really follow his own advice to a T. He wrote this while still single, and it didn't even REALLY work for him!"

"I read it as a teenager and bought into its message hook, line, and sinker. Now here I am, 25 years old and just learning how to pursue a woman for a relationship. This book has created an environment in churches where men literally try to figure out if they want to marry a woman before they ask them out to dinner or even coffee."

"Unfortunately, many well-meaning 20 somethings have tried to implement Harris' backward approach to dating and its resulted in young adults who don't have good relationship skills."

Though many in the church were commending Joshua Harris for sound guidelines on dating, just as many were accusing him of cult-ish practices and Pharisaical legalism.

I arrived late to the Christian dating scene post-Kissing-Dating-Goodbye, but I was under its influence for a while. Soon, I saw its polarizing effects. Tons of couples were blaming Joshua Harris and his ilk for all their relational anxiety. Every corner I turned, it seemed another pastor was counseling a marriage who couldn't get over feeling dirty or impure or irretrievably ruined.

Of course, everyone loves a good backlash. And Christians love to eat their own. There were a deluge of articles like "I Kissed Nonsense Goodbye" and "How Josh Harris Killed My Church" and "I Asked Out Dating Again." Christian bloggers were decrying courtship as a failed experiment and bashing Josh Harris on their blogs and podcasts with our typical Christianese fervor. If there's one thing I can count on from the church, it's a colorful outrage.

A few years ago, I decided to buy every single one of Joshua Harris's books. I wanted to get to the bottom of the whole thing. I was also suffering from some of the shackles of the dating subculture and feeling guilty myself. I had signed one of those Purity Contracts that told me, "No dating for a year," and I broke it in nine months (so close). I needed to know, "Was Josh Harris really to blame here?" But more importantly, *"Can anything good come out of all this?"*

I started with *Dug Down Deep,* Josh Harris's autobiography published in 2010. I quickly found that I really, really liked Pastor Josh. He was very dang likeable. He was a human being with the same hopes, dreams, and insecurities, like everyone else. I loved the relationship between him and his father. At one point Pastor Josh acknowledges that when his book unexpectedly hit it big, he became an arrogant, prideful person. By the end of the book, I felt like I had sat down with him over coffee, hearing his heart.

I know that a book can edit a person's own story to be more appealing. Maybe I was giving him too much credit. But cracking into his other work, I soon found another truth: that all his ideas weren't these atrocious tyrannical heresies. I didn't agree with all of them, but when do we ever? He had some wise things to say, and with enough discernment, I think the core remained good.

I learned something else along the way.

*The church culture can take a good idea and blow it up into a very, very bad idea.*

When the culture at large emphasizes a single aspect of an idea too long, it devolves into a **subculture**. A subculture is essentially a cyst that swells off the original intent of an idea. It's an out-growth, a near parody of itself amplified in its loudest traits. This is how you get angry partisan politics and watch-dog blog warriors and hateful picketers and shaky marriages built on false foundations.

This happens so easily. Someone can grab a quote out of context to support their own agenda and build an anti-dogma of binary anger. Each "side" of any argument can use the other side's quotes against them, until we're spiraling down a misinformed whirlwind of exaggeration and weaponized polemic.

It's hard to imagine that Josh Harris was concocting some evil scheme in his basement to guilt-trip the church. He couldn't possibly foresee how his ideas would mutate into the hyper-religious version we see today. I believe Pastor Josh is a God-centered man with his heart truly in a good place, but as with any social realm, a few of his ideas simply went out of control.

Here then, are Four Rational Thoughts about Christian books and their limitations.

I'm preaching to myself as I write this, too.

### 1) Nearly all Christian books presume a starting point of purity with no history, baggage, or brokenness.

There's an implicit stench of elitism in Christian literature which assumes all Christian readers are mid-20s, semi-attractive, upper-middle class suburbanites. Of course, this particular group needs Jesus too, and there's nothing wrong about that. But Christianese demographics assume a certain privilege and entitlement which is horrifically discriminating. While I doubt the authors intend this, often the book is living in a vacuum of non-consequence that won't speak on the behalf of the broken or abused.

The main fault here is: ***Being propositional*** *(working with ideals)* ***instead of relational*** *(working with people)* ***always leads to someone getting left behind.***[11]

When the preacher or author is inspiring us with ideals, everyone agrees. Jesus is good! Sin is bad! Watch your attitude! Repent now! No one disagrees with these unilateral statements. But I'm interested in *how our current reality can get to the ideal.* How do we get Heaven into the heartache?

I don't ever want to assume that the people I speak to are walking in with empty cups and a baggage-free life.

When the preacher is yelling about all the horrible things that will happen when you date, most of the room already knows how bad it gets. It's like showing that horrible car crash video in driver's ed class — it's a good reminder once in a while, but it doesn't teach me how to drive. We're already starting from a pretty messed up place before we can throw off the chains.

### 2) Christian books on dating mostly describe the consequences of dating.

Again, this is like describing the water I'm drowning in. I need to know how to swim.

When I lean in to love on someone, I don't want to tell them how they *should* be, but how they *could* be. I don't want them to live in a past of swirling shame, but to unlock them to a future of possibility empowered by God's grace.

Even if I warned you about every single consequence of dating, you'll *still* run into inescapable hurts that are simply just a part of being human.

The truth here is that life was never going to be easy. Even on our best days, we get entangled into unforeseen complications. We're constantly *in media res* from one season of mistakes to another, because life accumulates upon itself.

---

[11] Inspired by Donald Miller's *Searching For God Knows What.*

*Everything requires risk.* We can't shrink-wrap every decision or wear a helmet in our relationships (and if you do, high-five and let's hang out).

Whether you're sitting down or moving forward, life hurts.

Whether you're wallowing in pain or fighting for recovery, life hurts.

Healing hurts just as much as the original wound.

So we take the risk, any which way we go.

*("There is no safe investment. To love at all is to be vulnerable."[2])*

I'm not telling you to purposefully learn things the hard way. I'm not giving a permission slip to experiment with your own life or the fragile hearts of others. There are some things that are simply destructive the second you step to the line. If you're doing black tar heroin and chewing glass and pulling pins off grenades, I have to stop you.

Yet relationships always involve giving over the key of yourself, which inevitably leads to heated emotions, second-guessing, and self-doubt. Even the best relationships run into mixed signals, miscommunication, and ugly cry-face. Preventing every scraped knee will only hurt much worse when the real hurt comes.

I can't just tell you not to get hurt.

I want to be there in the aftermath.

We need a well-rounded approach that speaks to the pregnant teen, to the single mother working three jobs for her four kids, to the father who's dealing with his wife's affair, to the young lady who's been abused and molested. I believe Jesus is for these people, too, because they're people, and a person with problems is *never* a problem.

---

[2] C.S. Lewis, *The Four Loves* (New York: Harcourt, 1960, 1988) p. 121

**3) A culture built on the language of "Do's and Don'ts" and Reward/Punishment will only breed arrogance and add burdens.**

Whenever I see a post titled "7 Ways to Know How" or "What You Should Obviously Know" or "Don't Do This or You're A D-Bag" — I get a little knot in my guts and I'm compelled to tattoo all the info in my brainfolds. I feel both a mini-panic-attack and a bursting well of satisfaction that I suddenly know more than the helpless masses, because I got the secret sauce from Cracked and Buzzfeed and Relevant Magazine and Christianity Today, so I'm ready to flex my newfound skills to impress my unwitting friends.

Many of these practical tips are useful, maybe even life-saving. There are experts who have done it better than us, and we need to hear from them.

But again, such pragmatism either 1) paralyzes me into a deep fear of failure, or 2) gets me in an uppity self-righteous superiority over others who don't know.

I also get the sneaking suspicion that I'm just copying a programmatic method to earn the approval of my culture-bubble, and if I don't know the 20 Facts on What To Do When I'm 20, then I'm losing at life.

I can see the slithery snake of a needle underlying all these "Do's and Don'ts." We have suspected a secret insider-language suffocating every must-know list —

*You should. You're supposed to. You have to. You better — or else. If you miss this — you're out. Get on my program, or you're dead.*

I'm not sure this is any better than religion. It sounds like we're adding burdens rather than setting people free. And a list of "How To Set People Free" is still dripping with the poison of arrogance.

It's just adding rules about how to follow rules. This is *legalism,* and it's not okay.

thank you!

**4) Christian books can diagnose the problem, but cannot originate or motivate the Christian life.**

Christian media and Christian "celebrities" have great things to say, but *please don't fully trust them. Please don't trust me. Trust Jesus.*

A Christian book *can* tell you what's wrong and possibly tell you what to change.

A Christian book *cannot* cure what's really wrong and *cannot* make life-long change.

This is exactly how the Law of God works: it's to guide and expose our human condition, but it has no power to save you. Christian bestsellers are best at saying what's wrong, which is why they sell so much. Yet they can fall short on where to go next.

When I scramble to do the Study Guide or worksheet or end-of-chapter-questions of a Christian bestseller, it might inspire me for a time, but I'm only re-arranging my mental furniture. I'm going to forget a ton of that stuff because it can't take root with me. And I won't measure up to my small group or book club or accountability partner, because the moral standard I've been sold is an arbitrary goal-post that's coming from one broken person to another.

The Gospel — the Good News that a perfect God entered our fractured world to jumpstart the healing of all that is wrong — is *for the crushed who feel like it's too late for them.* It's for those who feel they're impure, tainted, or shattered. There's certainly a divine law and there are consequences for our bad choices, but God always begins in a place of rolling up His sleeves and diving into the mess we've made.

Something also has to compel us into an internally motivated, lifetime sustainable, inside-out life. Otherwise, all these "do's and don'ts" are just parole officers waiting for you to fail. They're bricks, all shape and no soul. We are plants, waiting for light and water to break in.

Life starts from the roots, from the pit, from the gut. It starts from a seed of unconditional acceptance, pushing through the dirt into the sun. Seeds have a law, but they're nourished by love.

Where everyone else and every other system demands I prove my smarts, my resume, my sexual prowess, my outgoing-ness, my ability to follow the three-points — there is a sacred space where I can quit selling myself. I can quit compensating for the wrong I have done. I am pre-approved here, qualified before I walk in the door. There is even acceptance here for legalists, for Pharisees, for those who burdened others with the rules they failed to keep themselves.

In this place, the rules are helpful, but they are not the ultimate measuring stick for my worth. They're not the be-all, end-all. They cannot tell me if I'm good enough or not enough. They help my behavior, but not who I am *becoming*. They only remind me that I fail, and they point to the one who doesn't.

I believe even in my darkest doubt that we are compelled by a *love who loves us before we did a single thing to prove our worth* and I'm free to walk into that love, with my gritty imperfections and messed up motives and my rough raw edges.

If the story of Jesus is true, that means:

*I can rest. I can relax. My motivation is not in gaining acceptance, but it starts in the acceptance He has already given. I can find resolve by knowing He resolved to find me first. I can fight, because He fought for me.*

We can quit getting antsy over do's and don'ts. We have room for our failures, we have another go, and in this we can succeed.

Here we move into this rest. Here we drink of His grace.
Here we can fight the good fight, too.

*rest in the here*
*that Jesus provides*

## *The Shoe Doesn't Always Fit, So Don't Force It*

So what about the weird things we do in Christianese Dating?

Do you enjoy writing letters to your future husband?

Do you like the idea of courtship and purity rings and dating contracts?

Do you read bestsellers about love languages and thought-talks and love dares?

Do you attend conferences about sex and dating and marriage and raising kids?

My friend: *all these things can be okay.* If they help, that's good. Really. Don't let anyone ridicule you for that. Don't let anyone belittle your convictions.

We can learn from them with discernment. If these things benefit you, go all the way.

If you cared enough to try any of these things, that in itself is a huge step in the right direction.

There are a ton of weird myths in the church-subculture about dating, but there are some good things too. It takes wisdom to sift through it, and a lot of humility, but when it works, it works. Life isn't just about romance, but there's plenty of romance in life to be ready for.

At the same time, I hope we can have *wisdom about our wisdom.*

We can get 1 John 4 on all that we read and hear.[13]

**There is no one-size-fits-all wisdom for relationships or the health of a couple.**

The purpose of this wisdom is always the same: to help love each other and love God on this journey of intimacy and support and life together. But the methods to promote the fruitfulness of this

---

[13] 1 John 4:1 – "Dear friends, do not believe every spirit, but test the spirits to see whether they are from God, because many false prophets have gone out into the world."

YES!

journey won't always be the Love-Tank or the 40 Day Love Challenge or the Purpose-Driven Marriage. If it helps, then go for it. If it doesn't, then toss it and we can arrive to a mutual method of self-giving love.

I've heard of dating couples who pray together to stay sane; I've heard of other couples who get tempted too much when they pray. Both are okay.

I've heard of dating couples who can play video games all night and they're not all hot and bothered; I've heard of other couples who choose not to be in the same room too long or they'll turn into sexual werewolves. Both are okay.

I've heard of couples who kiss and hold hands and hug until they get squished, and they don't spontaneously explode from lust; I've heard of other couples who keep constant arm-length and only do side-hugs because of their past. Both are okay.

I know some couples who are open and public and aim for marriage and get to know each others' families and it's all very serious; I know other couples who take it super-slow and stay on the down-low and it takes months or years for the parents to really come around. Both are okay.

Some couples date for a few years and realize it's the end, and they're cool about that. Some couples date for a few months and end it bitterly with high drama and sloppy emotions, and it takes a long time to recover. Both are okay.

Some people choose to stay single and celibate; some are simply not looking; because no one needs a romantic relationship to find romance, nor a significant other to find self-worth.

We can't really throw one blanket of dating advice for the wide spectrum of our individual personalities. Dating is like bringing two entirely different worlds into the same space, full of heat and chemistry and desire and history, so we seek the best way to mesh these worlds, and maybe there's a chance that it will turn into the gritty, messy, weird, wonderful thing we call love.

Each of us are wired with different longings, backgrounds, upbringings, and genetic history. Certain guidelines might be necessary for you because you'll need those safeguards to honor your partner and to honor God, and of course, to honor yourself. These kinds of boundaries will look unique for everyone.

For everyone who downright hates the high legalism of courtship, I want to suggest that the culture of courtship has some good ideas, and again, it's up to us to have discernment about them. I've heard pastors say, "Don't pick the meat from the bones, throw out the whole thing." Which means if any part of a book or sermon or advice is bad, then we toss it all out. And I understand that. Life is short; we can't waste all our time with bad teaching trying to find the good. But you know, *we do this all the time.* We watch advertisements this way. We watch movies and TV shows about despicable people without carrying their philosophies. We work with people who say the darndest things. You're already deciding whether to trust these words or not. While there are some impressionable people who won't question their beliefs, this is *more* reason to learn what works and what doesn't. As Aristotle reportedly said, *"It is the mark of an educated mind to be able to entertain a thought without accepting it."*[14]

When a preacher says, "Praying with the opposite sex is prayer-sex!" or "Dating and break-ups lead to unbreakable soul-ties!" — this is definitely shrill and a bit hilarious. Yet I understand the heart that led to such statements. They were not necessarily evil or altogether wrong. Inside these awfully hyper-religious declarations is a kernel of wisdom, and you may grow it into something better and more rounded, or shed it after some reflection.

---

[14] Attributed in Lowell L. Bennion, *Religion and The Pursuit of Truth* (Utah: Desert Book Co, 1959), p. 52

Of course, if you've been injured by any of these books or programs, then run. Do not look back. Be aware of overly religious strangle-holds. Share your story about your injury and about how it didn't work for you.

In the end, I can't really poke fun at these bestsellers. Some of them have valuable things to say; others are just hostility to the current state of things. But please do *not* buy into a simplified paradigm of romance. Please don't listen to either the uptight legalistic guilt-driven finger-pointer nor to the relaxed button-down casual hipster pastor.

It's between *you and God* to find your rhythm for romance, and God has gifted you with the freedom and discernment to evaluate the best way. It's in His grace that we can both relax and find resolve.

*"If anything has turned the world off to Christianity, it's the self-righteousness and arrogance that pretend our religious observance make us better than other people. But a Biblically informed view of indwelling sin and sanctification sweeps away self-righteousness. Christians who are being sanctified don't have time to be sanctimonious. They're aware of how far they have to go. They're aware of their weakness and God's ongoing grace toward them. This is what enables them to be gracious toward others."[15]*

— Joshua Harris

---

[15] Joshua Harris, *Dug Down Deep* (Colorado: Multnomah, 2001) p. 166

# Chapter 2.5
# Lust and Purity: The Brutally Honest Ugly Confrontation With Yourself

## *Purity Is Not A Trophy*

*"If anyone thinks that Christians regard unchastity as the supreme vice, he is quite wrong. The sins of the flesh are bad, but they are the least bad of all sins. All the worst pleasures are purely spiritual: the pleasure of putting other people in the wrong, of bossing and patronising and spoiling sport, and backbiting; the pleasures of power, of hatred. For there are two things inside me, competing with the human self which I must try to become. They are the Animal self, and the Diabolical self. The Diabolical self is the worse of the two. That is why a cold, self-righteous prig who goes regularly to church may be far nearer to hell than a prostitute. But, of course, it is better to be neither."*[16]
— C.S. Lewis

Every other week, there's another guy who approaches me and asks, *How did you quit porn? How do you handle lust? How do I stay pure?*

We talk about trigger warnings, accountability, a sobriety sheet, a clean streak, replacement behaviors, and battle plans.

All these are good, but when we only strive for the standard of "purity," we inadvertently leave God behind, which leaves us behind too.

Though we do fight to be pure:

[*Purity is not a trophy that you can fight for.*]

If your relationship or spiritual life is all about achieving a pure standard, you'll beat yourself up into miserable cycles of disappointment and defeat. I've been there, in that constant ricochet between patting myself on the back and beating myself up out of guilt. We then see our faith in terms of "clean" and "dirty." You'll

---

[16] C.S. Lewis, *Mere Christianity* (New York: HarperCollins, 1952, 1980), p. 103

constantly ask why you're not measuring up — and it's because you were never meant to.

Jesus preempted our failure at purity and everything else by taking our mess to the cross.

**Purity is a gift given by God.** It's *from* this gift, not for it, that we gratefully act upon God's life-giving law. Not because we're trying to earn anything, but because God has already begun to work His power through you. It's a tougher way, and often counter-intuitive: but it's better, and worth it.

If you can bask in the gift you've already received instead of striving to achieve it, then a healthy heart can follow. It will not be performance-driven self-righteousness, but other-centered and grace-empowered. It is both a pursuit *from* and a pursuit *forward* at the same time.

Rather than slaving away to destroy our own natural impulses, God has handed us the keys to His mansion and said —

*"You are clean already. You are invited. You are family. Now use this gift of purity for your maximum possible joy. Get to know the opposite sex for who they are instead of what they can give you. View them not as vehicles or obstacles, but human beings. You can have the best sex ever, in marriage, because this bond is forged by an ocean-deep commitment of lifelong promise as you travel through ups and downs on the greatest adventure of your life. That sort of sex will never be superficial or driven by performer's paranoia.*

*"You can do this because I have made you pure through My Son, I have declared you new, you're a re-creation, and I have set you free for joy. If you are single, that's okay. If you are lonely, don't fear. If you are struggling, I understand. I made you with this desire not to suppress you, but to pinpoint it for the exact purpose of divine intoxicating pleasure. It can be dangerous, but used My Way, it's about as close to Heaven as you can get."*

*↖ that's*

# *Fighting Lust Is Throwing A Pebble At A Waterfall*

There's a well-known story of a doctor in a village who was treating patients with busted legs. For days he kept seeing people with the same injury, and they all said the same thing. There was a pothole on the road, and on the way home, they would trip into it.

The doctor kept bandaging their legs, but eventually he had to take care of the pothole.

He did both. He offered the treatment and the remedy. One will cover, but the other gets to the very root.

When you begin to pull on the thread of lust, you find there are so many other ugly things intertwined. It might be easier just to learn the right behaviors, but really getting at the fiber of your own selfishness is horrible, humbling, humiliating work.

At times we'll take a common battle like *lust* and turn it into a dating issue instead of an identity issue. So most of us who are trying to overcome lust are just fighting our bodies to death in a grim hopeless war.

Attacking a symptom like this will only minimize the entire individuality of a whole person. Lust is simply one ingredient in the bigger pool of sexuality, and our microscopic view of the problem will poke at the wound but cannot treat the soul.

First you need to know: What we mostly experience as *natural impulse* is probably not lust, but just your hormones and desires and human design. There's nothing wrong with that, at all. We were made to have attraction and chemistry and romance and get married and have sex and make babies. To suppress that is to undermine our humanity, and God wants to make us more human and not less. We can relax a bit about our desires, because *all of us* will have a pulse of sexuality, which is part of who we are.

**Actual *lust* is when you're excessively orbiting around the objectification of a need or another person**. It's when natural desire becomes impersonal impulse. It's to consider flesh as your mental play-toy and physical receptacle. It uses and abuses. It dehumanizes. Lust is a vehicle for your ego.

In the infamous passage Matthew 5, when Jesus says, *"Anyone who looks at a woman lustfully has already committed adultery in his heart,"* he's not using the regular word for adultery. The specific word he chooses implies *greed*, a voracious appetite to fulfill the self. Right after, Jesus says, *"If your right hand causes you to sin, cut it off and throw it away. It is better for you to lose one part of your body than for your whole body to go to hell."* This is a superlative way of saying that 1) the continual greed for more is both a personal hell and can land you in the real one, and 2) our lust is not merely tied to our hands or flesh, but our entire being.

Lust is not just a bad organ that you can cut out of your body. It's indicative of a much bigger picture connected to all the areas of your life. It's wrapped up in who you are.

So many of us are trying to overcome over-sexualizing and porn addiction and fantasizing, but the bad news is: *we will fail.*

The thing about stopping lust is that we can't just "stop lust."

That's impossible. You might as well try to bite your ear or bench-press an airplane.

*Lust is not the problem, but a lack of direction.*

Once again: *This is not about better methods, but about where we're going.*

If you spend money like crazy, wake up in time for dinner, twist the truth to manipulate other people, show up late to everything, never listen to anyone, never put in effort anywhere, and push your agenda everywhere — then you will inevitably be a more lustful person. I would know, because I was like this.

**If you live an undisciplined life, I wouldn't expect that lust would be easy to control.** Whatever we choose to orbit, this fundamental axis will also determine our thoughts, behaviors, and attitudes. Each facet of your life is so interconnected that if you move one, the others must follow. When Apostle Paul talks about "fruits of the spirit" in Galatians 5, the word *fruit* is actually singular and not plural. It means even our goodness is interconnected, and that love cannot come without joy and peace and patience and kindness. Each of us are a wonderful collision of moving parts and variables that each depend on wholeness.

Lust then is really the default state of our lazy complacent drifting when we do what we want. It's a spendthrift detachment that fixes on self-centered pleasing, like dancing by yourself on a two foot stage. It's not about the sex or the porn, but your *pneuma*.

When we get this wrong, you've seen how this plays out.

If someone wants to quit porn while they're also first-world whiners and they're pursuing fleeting things, they don't have a chance.

If we keep saying "I'm a work in progress" — which is absolutely true of all of us — we're still neglecting the words *work* and *progress*.

And for the few decent people who get aggressive to quit, their recovery becomes their whole glory and they trade the idol of lust for the idol of conquest. Neither is better off, and we end up shooting ourselves in both feet.

So then, we can't just "fight lust."

There must be a direction, not to say "I finally defeated lust," but to move towards the powerful work that God wants to do through us.

Our self-control then is not merely running from lesser things, but to run towards all He has and is. **Repentance is not merely saying no to something, but saying yes to the best thing.**

When you grit your teeth and decide to quit porn, then you'll have idle free time and be bored out of your mind. Nine times out of ten, people go back to porn out of boredom. Or they just distract themselves with meaningless activities, but on the inside the lust is still reaching critical mass.

**The Christian life can't just be about running away from sin, but is ultimately about running to Him.** That means finding His mission, His purpose, and His heart for you. It means asking for His wisdom in how to discipline yourself, to be shaped by His truth, to be restructured in His image. It means bonding with other like-minded individuals to live out your God-given calling.

It's so fully experiencing the love of God that you are shaken down to your very core, melted and tenderized by His grace to never go back, but only pursue Him forward.

## *Defy Your Defiance: And Defy The Tacos*

*"You have an old self and a new self ... The old self is crippled with anxieties, the need to prove yourself, bad habits you can't break, and many besetting sins and entrenched character flaws. The new self is still you, but you liberated from all your sins and flaws. This new self is always a work in progress, and sometimes the clouds of the old self make it almost completely invisible. But sometimes the clouds really part, and you see the wisdom, courage, and love of which you are capable. It is a glimpse of where you are going.*

*"When Jesus' love, wisdom, and greatness are formed in us, each with our own unique gifts and callings, we become our 'true selves,' the persons we were created to be."[17]*

— Timothy Keller

My dear friend: the work of repentance will be absolutely painful. It's not just a one-time turn-around, but dying a thousand daily deaths to yourself. It's a good hurt, but it hurts.

---

[17] Timothy and Kathy Keller, *The Meaning of Marriage* (New York: Riverhead, 2011) pp. 132-133

The hard part is that we're so used to getting what we want. Our idea of God always gets put on the shelf when we're tempted into the path of least resistance.

Most privileged entitled Westerners have access to just as much as we want, when we want it, in total privacy. I know that makes me sound like an old-fashioned preacher here, but really: we're floating in excess. And that's not entirely your fault.

If you want tacos at three in the morning, then by God, you will get those tacos. Every street in America has a Taco-Something with any filling you could imagine: fried steak, chocolate ice cream, cheese-covered ramen. Nothing is stopping you. It's not a sin. I do that more than I'd like to admit. I think tacos taste better while other people are sleeping.

Occasionally though, when I'm up late and I'm craving that burrito preñado with cochinita pibil from Taco Bus, I just tell myself, *No.*

Not every time. *But I need to know how to say no to myself.* Most of us hardly ever do that. It's not natural to defy ourselves.

It doesn't make me a better Christian. I get no sense of superiority. This is not "character-building." I don't suddenly think of Jesus when I say no to enchiladas. I suppose this sounds like a fundamentalist thing to do, and I don't recommend it to everyone.

I say this to tell you: *Whenever I say no to myself, it's embarrassingly hard.*

And I recognize my garish dependence on free access to everything.

I've actually dreamed of tacos when I didn't get one. That succulent, red, juicy salsa pouring from the mouth of that burrito. I actually try to sleep faster so time will go quicker and then I can have a taco during the day time like a regular human person. And when I say no to myself the night before, the next day I always order two. For myself.

It's all rather silly, and I'm not trying to correlate this too closely with lust. I'm saying that my craving for tacos can get disturbing. Fighting an appetite exposes so much entrenched entitlement and greed. I end up hating myself for being so weird and selfish. I get threatened by knowing I'm never as good as I think I am. As C.S. Lewis says,

*"No man knows how bad he is till he has tried very hard to be good. A silly idea is current that good people do not know what temptation means. This is an obvious lie. Only those who try to resist temptation know how strong it is."*[18]

So I must defy myself to face the monster inside.

I must be able to say, "I'm onto you."

I must challenge the creatures in my basement.

And if it hurts to defy something like tacos, I must be ready for the anguish of real, deliberate, reconstructive soul-surgery.

My friend, it won't be pretty. Giving up our old life is like amputating a limb. Getting on God's mission is intimidating. Sitting down with a pastor or your friend to confess the things in our basement requires a vulnerability that we don't want to risk. Relinquishing my ego always makes me howl in agony. We will mess this up, a lot. There will be so many chains to unravel. We'll sometimes fall back into the lesser things. We'll think we're making progress but run into some embarrassing setbacks, and we'll question if we've really changed at all.

*It's an ugly battle to confront your own ugliness.* We're used to the complacency of our status quo and it will sometimes feel like clawing out of a pit. It's an uphill fight every day.

But if you can start this climb: I'm so excited for you, my friend.

This is where God meets us to do His best work.

I hope we're willing to let God press in on us, to contradict us, to confront us.

---

[18] C.S. Lewis, *Mere Christianity* (New York: HarperCollins, 1952, 1980), p. 143

**When we can confront ourselves truly as we are in the all-revealing presence of God, we can begin to be liberated from the lies we believe.** We can see where we were just fooling ourselves. Such a confrontation is completely uncomfortable and downright agonizing, but afterward, we can be free. The chains loosen. There is clarity. There is joy. Honesty is freedom.

Whatever you need to let go of and whatever you need to start, you already know what it is. Don't be afraid to be honest. By the grace of God, you can begin today.

*"Who am I? What is my 'self'? The answer is that I am a Jekyll and Hyde, a mixed-up kid, having both dignity because I was created and have been re-created in the image of God, and depravity because I still have a fallen and rebellious nature. I am both noble and ignoble, beautiful and ugly, good and bad, upright and twisted, image and child of god, and yet sometimes yielding obsequious homage to the devil from whose clutches Christ has rescued me. My true self is what I am by creation, which Christ came to redeem, and by calling. My false self is what I am by the Fall, which Christ came to destroy."*[19]

— John Stott

---

[19] John Stott, *The Cross Of Christ* (Leicester: Inter-Varsity, 1989) p. 285

# Chapter 3
# The Scary Anxious Pursuit of "The One"

*"People get from books the idea that if you have married the right person you may expect to go on 'being in love' forever. As a result, when they find they are not, they think this proves they have made a mistake and are entitled to a change — not realising that, when they have changed, the glamour will presently go out of the new love just as it went out of the old one. In this department of life, as in every other, thrills come at the beginning and do not last. The sort of thrill a boy has at the first idea of flying will not go on when he has joined the R.A.F. and is really learning to fly. The thrill you feel on first seeing some delightful place dies away when you really go to live there. Does this mean it would be better not to learn to fly and not to live in the beautiful place? By no means. In both cases, if you go through with it, the dying away of the first thrill will be compensated for by a quieter and more lasting kind of interest. What is more (and I can hardly find words to tell you how important I think this), it is just the people who are ready to submit to the loss of the thrill and settle down to the sober interest, who are then most likely to meet new thrills in some quite different direction. The man who has learned to fly and become a good pilot will suddenly discover music; the man who has settled down to live in the beauty spot will discover gardening.*

*"This is, I think, one little part of what Christ meant by saying that a thing will not really live unless it first dies. It is simply no good trying to keep any thrill: that is the very worst thing you can do. Let the thrill go — let it die away — go on through that period of death into the quieter interest and happiness that follow — and you will find you are living in a world of new thrills all the time."*[20]

— C.S. Lewis

---

[20] C.S. Lewis, *Mere Christianity* (New York: HarperCollins, 1952, 1980), p. 111

*"When you stop expecting people to be perfect, you can like them for who they are. And when you stop expecting material possessions to complete you, you'd be surprised at how much pleasure you get in material possessions. And when you stop expecting God to end all your troubles, you'd be surprised how much you like spending time with God."*[27]

— Donald Miller

## *Check Your Reality: The Subterranean Underbelly of Waking Life*

After one of my friends went on a two-week mission trip to a third world country, he tells me, "I would totally love to live there!" — and I had to rain on his parade, because I really wanted him to understand the gravity of what he was saying.

I hate to be the guy that does the "Reality Check," because that guy is never fun.

But really, we have a propensity for over-romanticism in our hyper-sentimental culture, and when reality meets expectations, we get disillusioned and jump ship. I've seen it happen all the time: in marriages, in parenting, in careers, in church. A poor estimation of the daily grit of life will always cause us to check out and quit too early.

This is a prevalent pattern in a world of five-minute ramen and eight minute abs – we run out at the first sign of trouble. It gets easier to do this each time, until we're jumping from one half-committed island to another.

Living in a third world country and serving the poor is hard work. *Very* hard work. It's easy to go on a two-week mission trip and Instagram the perfect moments and bring back the slideshow to

---

[21] Donald Miller, *A Million Miles In A Thousand Years* (Tennessee: Thomas Nelson, 2009) p. 206

your church (I've done it too). [But a mission trip is a dip in the water compared to the daily effort of swimming upstream with real hurting people.]

When you see a two hour "chick flick" and get to the Happily Ever After, none of this reflects the truth of romance and the everyday ordinary choices to persevere. Romance looks easy on TV when the onscreen protagonists steal a smirking wink, and this can easily awaken a premature longing in us that doesn't estimate the high cost of love. Children are cute until they're screaming in your face for the toy in Aisle 5. Old married couples look cute until you hear about their fifty years of pain, arguments, lying, betrayals, forgiveness, and the long nights of loneliness in the same bed.

War and fame and traveling all look pretty cool in movies until you're there in the field, sweating down your shorts and pushing through crowds and squinting in the sun. Our over-romanticism, the *Glorification of Intoxication,* is a deception that works because there's just enough to truth to bait us. There's just enough surface beauty to seduce us into passive participants, waiting for my entitled life to unfold. We fall for the photoshopped version of things.

I'm not endorsing a stoic cynicism or a jaded detachment here. I'm jaded to that, too. Nothing is wrong with high standards or even high expectations. It's just that these will only tell half the story. It's an incomplete picture that we expect to complete the picture in our heads. Real life involves a lot of sweaty armpits, standing around in line, sending texts with embarrassing typos, coughing really weird at the wrong moment, pulling out wedgies when no one notices, and the constant waiting for the next best thing to happen.

This Idealistic Romanticizing is prone to take shortcuts, cut corners, and demand success the moment an endeavor begins. I've spoken with so many new bloggers who are excited to be the next viral hit, and while I hope they always hit it big, they get discouraged in the first week when there are no views or likes or comments. And

I have to wonder if they were only blogging for attention. They quit after a few weeks and end up devaluing their self-worth.

Do you remember the first time you wrote a song on the guitar or piano, and you were so excited to share with your best friend? You sat them down and played the song for them. About halfway through the second verse, it begins to feel very clumsy and insecure. There's a moment you want to quit, but you're already building up to the second chorus with your slightly different vocal flourishes. Your friend is sort of waiting for you to finish up and you're both making really weird eye contact while you sing the high notes of the bridge. When you're finished and you sheepishly ask, "What did you think?" — your friend is not exactly sure what to say, except, "Cool. I'm going to shower now and order a pizza."

That's it, right there. That's the whole bizarre discomfort of waking up to life. We simply need to finish the song. Then maybe order a huge gross pizza.

## Kill The Honeymoon

When someone has an idea for a business, for charity, for a church, for a novel or art or an invention: all these things are great. Yet there's a depth to all these things, a kind of marathon endurance that pushes past the emotional spark of grandeur. When the fun of beginning is over, then there's an actual finish-line ahead of us.

When a young dude tells me, "I would really like to be a pastor" – I'm always the jerk to give the gut-check. I'm the harbinger of bad news and the crusher of dreams. I end up saying, "No you're not ready" a lot of the time, and usually the response is, "You're just a hater, you don't know me man, God's gonna use me." I've hurt a lot of fragile egos who weren't willing to undergo the honesty of self-examination, including me. I've been cussed out or cut off. But really, I want to give an honest accurate view of what pastoral ministry is like, what *life* is like. If I don't, then I wouldn't be a good friend or a good pastor. I say this with as much love and grace as possible *but so long as you do not correctly estimate the sweat and blood and tears of where you're headed,* the lack of seriousness will deplete the life of everyone involved. Then when you no longer "like it" or "want it," you'll mentally check out or you'll run off and do more damage.

My fiancé and I probably look cute in pictures (her much more than me), and maybe our story would give you a false idea that it was "love at first sight" and it somehow fell into place. We've been together six years, and I still have a crush on her like it was the first week. Yet most of our six years was effort upon grace upon sacrifice. At the three-year mark, we had broken up for six months because we were sure it was over. We found our way around again, painfully, through many brutally honest conversations, and this is the shape of everyday love.

My dear friend: **The honeymoon has to end.**

The start is the easy part.

We begin things well. It's hard to finish strong.

It's good to get excited, but excitement must give way to a deeper, truer pulse.

If you can persevere past the naïve burst of beginning —

We can expand our wonderful first memories into a beautifully woven story.

**Preparing for what's to come is really half the battle.** When we know that life requires the very best of us, we can count the cost and put in our all. When we can have a self-awareness that dating and relationships are not the all-fulfilling dream we've hyped them up to be, then we can actually be ready for the lifelong challenge of forbearance and intimacy. When you know that this roller coaster is longer than two minutes and three turns, then you can cherish the highs and brace yourself for the lows.

When we quit expecting relationships to look like Hollywood, we can actually enjoy them for what they are. We can get to know the person in all their ragged edges, not for who we want them to be, but for their wounds and worries and scars.

## *What To Expect While You're Expecting ... And That Baby Voice*

Relationships are a lot more embarrassing and gritty than we would like to admit. When I hear a glamorous story about how a couple fell into each other's arms, I'm absolutely sure that's *not* how it happened.

No one wants to talk about the Baby Voice.

If or when you start dating, you'll have a certain kind of voice over the phone. It's the Baby Voice. You'll sound like an eight year old goober. When my fiancé and I are in our private moments, we have a completely different inflection than in public, and sometimes when we're out in the real world, we giggle at each other's "Public Voices" because they're so deep and official.

To get more serious, no one wants to talk about the regretful text messages or the immature arguments or the tactless yelling over the art of arguing. The first fart. The long stream of farts from then on forever. Crusty-eyed drool face. The pre-makeup face. Cry-face. Yawn-face. The obnoxious hyper-moments when you apparently lose control of your civilized body and do puppet shows and movie impressions. The silences when you're not sure what to talk about as you hear the croutons smushing between your teeth.

None of these things are worth putting in a movie (with the single exception of *When Harry Met Sally* and the infamous croutons smushing between the teeth). And each of these things become routine, part of the package, the not-so-cute parts you never saw coming.

Soon you'll encounter all the crustiness of a real person.

Eventually, everyone "falls out of like." You'll be in the direct space of all a person's grossness, including your own. As Tim Keller says, *"Finally, you have nowhere to run."*[22]

When the romanticized feelings go: where do we go from there?

When the electric current you first felt is gone, the only things that can rightly take over are *commitment* and *covenant.* It's a **daily choice** to give yourself over to a promise, no matter what you might be getting out of it, because what you're getting out of it is merely the beauty of the thing you committed to in itself.

This all sounds overly romantic too, but in practice it's probably the most difficult thing you'll ever do. Commitment truly requires your *everything.*

So who would ever want to do this? Who is even capable?

The awesome truth is that **there's not a whole lot better than the confident security and vulnerability of an exclusive covenantal commitment.** There's nothing quite like coming home to find home with your loved one. This is why even in an increasingly post-marriage culture, we *still* celebrate fifty-year marriages. We cheer for dreams that go the distance. We're still not a people that celebrates running away or cutting things short or quitting halfway through. No one is popping a champagne bottle over half a built bridge.

God designed us this way, but even better, *God gives us the power to do what He envisions.* The power of commitment comes from both the commitment itself and the Grand Author of such a binding. A covenant has a lifetime richness that first begins with the surface-attraction of a rushing river, but eventually fills out with the depth of a great ocean.

As G.K Chesterton said,

*"Love is not blind; that is the last thing that it is. Love is bound; and the more it is bound the less it is blind."*[23]

---

[22] Timothy Keller, "Marriage As Commitment and Priority," September 1st 1991

And I hope that we're not too eager to run out on this.

It doesn't mean we look for instant loyalty at the first hint of a goal. It doesn't mean we're looking for marriage whenever romance begins. It means that once we take the risk, we're ready for all the sloppy, goofy, slobbery, strange intricacies of our journey. It means that we do not force people into the hologram we've imagined in our heads.

It means letting God do the work only He can do: to re-create us into a deeper people, living truly from our hearts, as the people He has saved us and made us to be.

It's never easy, but by God, is it ever glorious.

*"I was talking with my friend's mom tonight and after she told me she and her husband are about to celebrate their 30th anniversary, I asked her what the key to having a successful marriage is. This was her answer:*

*"Two pioneers in separate ships reach the same piece of land. They decide that together, they can make it on this land with each other. They don't know what all they'll come across since it's new territory, but they swear to each other that they'll take it one day at a time and face it side-by side, so they burn their ships and they burn the port. That's how you make marriage work. You choose who you want to face it all with, and then you decide that leaving is not an option. You have to both burn your own ships."[24]*

— Lauren Britt

The following are seven questions from real people about navigating our pursuit of a relationship. Nothing here needs to be memorized nor formulized, but will hopefully inform your own process of discovering the grit in romance. As always, please feel free to skip around.

---

[23] G.K. Chesterton, *Orthodoxy* (Chicago: Moody, 1908, 2009), p. 108

[24] Lauren Britt, "Burn Your Ship,"
http://yesdarlingido.tumblr.com/post/99379507440/burn-your-ship

### 1. Can A Guy and Girl Be Friends?

"I know there is no straight up answer to this question because everyone has different boundaries and it's a matter of permissible vs. beneficial. I've made a lot of mistakes in the past which have resulted in a lot of hurt and drama. What are some healthy guidelines for emotional boundaries in opposite gender friendships? How can I pursue a healthy, deep and 'intimate' friendship while guarding my heart (and the other person's) without being legalistic? Or can guys and girls not be close friends?"

Here's the short, simple answer on this one:

While everyone thinks they can beat the odds and be the exception, almost *no one* can escape romantic feelings if they have a super-intimate relationship with the opposite gender.

The important thing here is **what you choose to do with those feelings**.

In other words: You have a right to feel what you feel, but you're not obligated to pursue it *(Just because you feel romantic emotions, does not inevitably lead to a date and a wedding.)*

I know this probably isn't your motive, but it's so ingrained in us today that boys and girls can only flirt to communicate and there's all this "unrequited longing" that we emulate from sitcoms.

I'm reminded of a very poignant Simpsons episode[25] where Homer has feelings for another woman, so he thinks he *has* to have sex with her. He actually starts sobbing in his hands and says, "We're gonna have sex." I died from the laughter and profoundness.

Because of our overly sexualized culture, we assume that being around the opposite gender immediately means "romantic possibilities," but it does *not*. You and I learned that from bad rom-coms, Hollywood saturation, and your over-sexed group of friends.

---

[25] http://youtu.be/DNZmqtzoYaY?t=45s

We've all bought into "friend-zone" frenzy, but no one is entitled to a date just because they're "nice." We live in quite an impulsive impatient generation, so we assume our first instinct must be the right one — as if we need to chase the rabbit every time. I might sound like an eighty year old preacher about to fall off the pulpit, but really, if I didn't love you, I would tell you to go to hitherto with your heart like everyone else is telling you to do.

My friend, you know your boundaries already. Do you know how you know? Because you've been hanging out with friends since you could walk. You learned how to navigate your own personality, the art of communication, your preferred space, whether you were an extrovert or introvert, and what kind of things you like to do. You don't need to suddenly change all the rules for the opposite gender. Why would you?

I'm sure you see this playing out the wrong way all the time. We all know the guy who suddenly changes his voice and puffs out his chest when a girl walks in. We all know the girl who gets shrill and obnoxious when a dude walks in. No one actually thinks it's cute.

I'm not talking about the natural nervousness of being around someone we're attracted to. I mean that many of us are subconsciously trapped by trying to impress the opposite gender, as if maybe something will happen out of thin air. And very few people actually question how we got to this mutant form of romance.

We all need to relax about this and realize **we are much more than our sexuality.** [We are human beings who share the common need for companionship and authenticity and intimacy, with both genders, and we can leave it at that without making it some drama. We can be grown-ups about this. ]

Please don't believe the lie of immature romance. Yes, a guy and a girl can be friends, if you can just quit believing that feelings *have* to go somewhere. They don't.

(If you meet an awesome person chasing after Christ and you hit it off and there are fireworks, then hey, go for it. Again, dating is not some evil monster that will ruin your future marriage. Too much of the Christian subculture on dating throws around false guilt for bad decisions when the church never taught us how to date wisely in the first place.)

If or when you get married, you'll pretty much phase out most opposite-gender friends anyway. It happens naturally. I know that sounds unfair and someone always thinks they can beat this, but you can't really tell your wife, "Okay honey, I'm hanging out with Amy today, k thx bye!" Spouses who don't draw these lines out of pride end up getting into disastrous trouble. Not unless you like sleeping by the front door. And trust me, when you're mature enough to consider marriage, then leaving behind some of those friends will actually feel like a good thing.

So please set your boundaries by the ones you already have for friendship, investigate your own heart on what's comfortable for you, and relax around the boys and girls. If you feel your heart racing, just thank God you're alive and you have the privilege of those emotions. It doesn't mean you have to act on it: *you* make that choice.

*"It's important for little girls to know not every story has to be a love story and for boys to know that soldiers aren't the only ones to triumph in war."*
— Guillermo del Toro

*what a wonderful way to look at it*

## 2. What To Look For In A Future Spouse?

**"What do you look for in a future partner/spouse? I ask because I really have trouble with this. I am a female, but even if I find a Godly male I worry that it is going to damage in my relationship with God, opposed to good. Probably because I've been in a idolatrous relationship where the other ended up poorly influencing me, instead of the other way around. I also seem to miss out on warning signs."**

I understand the sensitivity of the question and it's most likely from good curious motives, but I'm very wary of the Wishlist type of thinking that has pervaded modern dating. Even —gasp!— in our churches.

I once had a Wishlist too. I was attracted to loud, aggressive, hot, fiery, dominant women. Seven dead relationships later with plenty of heartbreak and nightmare scenarios, I realized the stupidity of looking for a "type." Like Tim Keller says, since people change, "you always end up marrying the wrong one" anyway.[26] When you find a type and hope the type will last, it's never a stable guarantee. People are known to have major life changes approximately every seven years, so you're a new person at least ten times in your life.[27]

Certainly there is room for physical attraction, common goals, and spiritual compatibility. But your main concern right now should be you. As Francis Chan says, if your future spouse becomes your air supply to meet your needs (instead of God being the air supply), you will both drown each other.[28] God must be your first lover and foundation. Those who are ready for marriage are the ones who need it least.

---

[26] Timothy Keller, *The Meaning of Marriage* (New York: Dutton, 2011), 38.
[27] For more on that concept, check out Michael Apted's "Up Series," which has documented a group of people from seven years old every seven years. The series is currently at 56 years old.
[28] Francis Chan and Lisa Chan, "Christ-Centered Relationships Part 1" (preached at Cornerstone Simi Valley Church) July 27, 2008.

It's very possible that the idolatry you entered was not entirely your fault, since many men can be brash, act-tough-to-cover-shortcomings, and usually date a girl to fulfill their selfish hormonal desires. But it's also possible that men became the filler for your walk with God, so that dating simply revealed what was already in your heart, or what was not there at all.

The best thing is **make friends first**. Your really good friends of the same sex were *discovered* and not found (brought to you by C.S. Lewis). In other words, you didn't have to force it and there was a reasonable pace on your journey to being friends. With romance we tend to go so fast that we skip a billion important steps of growth and that's when damage happens.

When you find that guy-friend who doesn't fake it, isn't trying to impress you, and is helping you walk with God instead of helping you drown — just like *a real friend does* — then consider a cup of coffee. Don't rush, do have a good time, and don't ever be afraid to tell him no.

wow, if only I had advice like this on the daily

### 3. Why Save Myself For Marriage?[29]

- "Hi there! Can you explain to me what's so great about marriage and saving myself? Won't I be missing out on having sex with other people?"

- "Pastor Park, I am Christian as is my boyfriend. We are older and I have told him from the start that I do not want to engage in sexual intercourse before marriage. He seemed fine with it but every now and then pressures and or guilts me by saying that everyone does it but us. We have friends who are Christian and do it themselves but I cannot bring myself to do it. How can I convince him in a Christian manner that I do not want to because I think it is a sacred act?"

Hey dear friends: So this is a very complicated issue that I know the world increasingly pushes away as old-fashioned moralism. I understand that most people will not see eye-to-eye on anything the Bible has to say about sex, and it's in fact the very reason that most visitors think the church is an out-of-touch institution that polices our behavior.

But I strongly believe the more we look into God's plan for us, the more it will make sense at the logical, emotional, physical, and spiritual level. If we can really think through why God would even give us this vision, I believe it will win as the most sensible option.

Before making objections like "What about ___?" — please at least consider that *fasting from sex until marriage could certainly work out for the mental and emotional health of the couple.* It's easy to just buy into the societal "norm" about sex and shrug off the Bible on this area, but I've seen (and been through) too many miserable sexual disasters to not at least speak up, because I love you even at the cost of sounding archaic and not-cool.

---

[29] This is also in my book *What The Church Won't Talk About,* available on Amazon.

I know many will disagree quickly and say, "Sex and morality are two separate issues." While I do believe sex has a moral dimension, I also believe it's equally an issue of *wisdom*. When the church says the phrase *sexual sin*, it sounds very hokey and eye-rolling, but really it means any kind of sexual expression which goes against God's goodness for us, therefore causing profound harm and relational breakdown. (*Sin always goes against God's best*) and it will leech the life and joy right out of us. God would only give us these sort of commands for a broken world if He knew the trouble that sex could cause — and if He also knew the best way to find maximum joy through it.

Sex has the power to be either the most destructive or most joyful thing in the world.[30] However you feel about the modern state of Christianity, I very much hope we can consider hearing (and following) what the Bible has to say about sex. Please consider that most of us already have a predisposed bias to shutting this out as crazy church talk. Whether we admit it or not, we have a vested interest in wanting to have mindless intercourse. So maybe we can drop our biases, even for a moment. (God loves you and cares for you in this area, regardless of how the church fumbled the message. The heart of God is *for* you, and for *you.*)

So a question upfront: **What else would we expect the God who loves us and knows what's best for us to say about sex?** What would a loving father say to his thirteen year old daughter? What would a loving mother say to her son? In fact: what would a fifteen year old brother tell his twelve year old sister?[31]

*A side-note:* If you're being pressured into sex that you don't want, please immediately draw safe boundaries and enforce your dignity as loudly as possible. Any unwanted sexual advance that violates your space is classified under sexual assault, and it's a crime. Be willing to

---

[30] Inspired by Timothy Keller. Check out his book *The Meaning of Marriage.*
[31] Inspired by Andy Stanley's sermon series, "Love, Sex, and Dating."

remove yourself from that situation, even permanently, and to alert the authorities.

*Another side-note:* I'm not the most qualified person to write on this because I've struggled with it my whole life. But by God's grace, I've grown very much in this too.

### 1) Premarital sex causes confused intimacy.

Physical sex was designed to bring a husband and wife closer together, to re-create and renew the exclusive covenant bond, to be absolutely vulnerable and give-all with one another.

When it's done outside marriage, it will make you feel closer to the person than you really are. Several pathologies result. You will bypass the biblical pace of intimacy — discovery, sharing, encouraging, prayer, self-control, honor, respect — and build a false connection on physicality. Any time you bypass God's commands, you'll soon become a half-formed, unrealized, virtual copy of yourself. Because God's commands are *how things work.*

Since premarital sex has no guarantee of long-term commitment (and even if it did), any real intimacy is short-circuited by a pride to protect yourself or a desperation to "win" that person. So people break up like disposing trash or they stay much longer in a relationship than they should for the wrong reason. In church we call that *bondage.*

*Objection: "What about trying out a person to see if they're the right fit?"* Please know that this immediately dehumanizes a person into a shoe or a car. People are not shoes and cars. If a man came home with your daughter and said, "I need to test-drive her for a while, see if the sex is what I want" — how would you respond?

For some reason, *women always become abused property when we have no guidelines for sex.* In any nation's history, this has always been true. That should tell us something about "sexual freedom." In a place where people leave sex unchecked, inevitably women always end up objectified, diminished, and tossed around like chattel.

If you think you're "missing out on sex with other people," I can tell you from firsthand experience that this is a baseless thought with zero grounding in reality. Romantic intimacy is best when it's an exclusive promise to be faithful to one another for life. When you have this kind of security and safety, you can fully let yourself go into the kind of relational trust that we've all been looking for.

## 2) God shapes the vision of your spouse's beauty on *one spouse.*

First Corinthians 7:3-4 touches on this. As one pastor said, Adam only had one spouse and one vision of beauty: "It's either Eve or aardvark." Adam didn't practice physical prowess with anyone else, nor did he have a catalogue to compare. When you have multiple pictures of so-called beauty in your life, it's almost impossible to be satisfied with one wife or a million.

It's quite a tragedy when we can never be satisfied with consistent stability. This is why porn is so destructive to marriages. It destroys a man's desire for his wife when he has a buffet-mentality. Again, the culture still celebrates fifty-year marriages for this very reason: because the husband and wife dedicated themselves to one wonderful vision.

*Objection: "What if I don't want to get married and I'm just fine sleeping around the rest of my life?"*

I'm just wondering if we're all okay with settling for a cheap imitation of the real thing. I know that sex is hard *not* to do because it's good. Of course it's good, and God knows that.

This is where we must look forward instead of looking back. I could tell you all the reasons why premarital sex is immoral, but let's instead see God's better plan.

When you have the covenant blessing of God, a commitment made in front of all parents and friends and family, a legal union made public to the world, a heart promised to your spouse forever, a bed that will only have one lover for life, a mind that is full of your spouse's body as the standard for your desire, and the loving devotion of your spouse to sanctify and encourage and rebuke and know you as you really are — imagine that sort of sex. *It's the best sex imaginable.* Anything else is a low budget, laughable, poorly assembled knock-off.

I also think celibacy is a great viable option if you're called into God's mission for a specific reason. But it's very rare. Declaring celibate status out of resentment for relationships won't work out. It's really for those commissioned for something unique, like Jesus or Apostle Paul or Mother Teresa.

> *"Real love, the Bible says, instinctively desires permanence."*[32]
> — Timothy Keller

### 3) There are psychological ramifications of premarital sex that are impossible to ignore.

I know this will sound like heavy-handed preacher-talk, but if you're having premarital sex, whether with a random person or your fiancé, it exposes a lack of discipline and self-control. In general: *a lack of control now only explodes in marriage and in life.* We bring all our problems forward, including that one. If you're not good at budgeting, don't clean well, raise your voice a lot, punch walls, and don't like children, none of that will get cured by marriage or getting older.

I understand this is ridiculously hard to accept in a world of impulse and access. Today, there's almost no gap between *urge* and *gratification.* If you want tacos at two in the morning, by God, you'll

---

[32] Timothy and Kathy Keller, *The Meaning of Marriage* (New York: Riverhead, 2011) p. 90

get them. If you get feelings for your opposite-gender friend, we automatically fool ourselves into thinking "I need to be with her" instead of realizing *we don't need to chase our feelings every time they happen to us.* Most of it is just hormones stirring in your pants. If you're one of the 39% of people in the world who have the internet[33], then nothing is stopping you from stealing a movie, cheating on your homework, or watching porn. In our Westernized whip-fast climate, we presume this is how life should work: at my fingertips, at my bidding, whatever I want, whenever I want it.

I hate to sound like an alarmist. And I don't believe that we need to become an ascetic vegan monk who lives in a temple made of home-made hemp (which actually sounds fun). But all this entitlement and privilege and affluence can only distort our desires and drunken us with power. We're an entertained generation of instant delivery. Try to remember the last time you told yourself, *No.* It's probably been longer than you think.

*Objection: "I already gave in so I might as well keep doing it."*
Here's what so great about the God of the Bible.

He never, ever, ever calls it too late to turn away from unwise decisions and to trust in His goodness for you. *God never says it's too late to turn from your sin and trust in Him.*

Certainly there will be some consequences for choices we have made. But that's true for everyone. No one walks around with a baggage-free life, and God can work with that.

I've talked with too many people (including myself) who regret so many past grievances in their sexuality — and I'll go as far to say that *most peoples' major regrets in life have to do with their bodies and expressions of sexuality.* They feel hopeless, dirty, beyond redemption, used up, with a give-in sort of resignation.

This is where God always meets us with grace and restoration and the gift of a new start. You might have tons of guilt and shame

---

[33] http://www.internetworldstats.com/stats.htm

over this, *but Jesus died for that very reason, to offer grace and healing for all the ways you've messed up.* When you believe that, God calls you pure and new when the world says otherwise, when even you say otherwise. God calls you clean when no one else will.

(We begin to understand that purity is not something you fight for, but a gift that God gives you so that you'd fight *from* it.) God can rewire your old patterns of thinking, and much of that begins by simply knowing *you are now an adopted, re-created, bought-with-a-price child of God in Christ.* It's hard to think with your old patterns when you know the price that was paid on the cross and how much God sincerely wants you to be free from everything that hurts you.

*[handwritten: honestly, I'd not]* (not that I've done that for those borrowing)

You'll also discover the sanctity of really getting to know a person beyond their physical chemistry.

If you're a dude, I can almost guarantee that your girlfriend would be absolutely thrilled if you told her, "Babe, I want to save ourselves for marriage now. I'm really sorry about before. I respect that you're a God-created human being and not just a body. I want to get you know you for who you really are."

If you're a lady, I can almost guarantee that if your boyfriend told you this, then you found a keeper, and every other dude would look like a scrub.

My friend, I encourage you to please keep seeking the answer on this one for yourself. For those who are committed to wait: I know it's tough and it won't be a perfect process, but please don't let that be an excuse either. God will give you the grace to fight for your dignity. God will restore your purity from the past too. I've barely scratched the surface on this, and I pray you find that *sex within marriage is the best possible sex you could ever have.* Anything else by comparison, is no comparison.

## 4. Seven Thoughts On Singleness: Is Something Wrong With Me?

"I'm 27 years old and I've never had a boyfriend. I've only dated once but that didn't go so well. I've prayed and I've prayed and I've asked God for my significant other but honestly sometimes I feel as if God doesn't hear me. Which then causes my heart turmoil especially when I see other girls getting married and dating all the time. It just makes me feel like there is something wrong with me or I maybe I'm unworthy of someone else. I just really need some peace in this area or my life."

Hey dear sister, I know this is an especially painful season for you right now, but please allow me the grace to share a few thoughts with you.

### 1) Singleness is not a season of waiting.

I've said this before, but: *You're not waiting for a man. A man is not the focal point of anything. Jesus is the focal point of everything.*

A Western culture indoctrinated in romanticism would lead us to believe that "singles" are simply biding their time, waiting for some significant other to save us from the throes of loneliness. And I know that the latest pop song or chick flick or young adult novel has awakened some weird feelings in you, and it would even be nice to have someone.

But relationships are hard work, celibacy is hard work, and *life* is hard work. There's really no such thing as waiting for a spouse: your life has launched into being, and there's work to do. [If God is your priority, then a man who comes along who can even catch up to you would be dang lucky to have you.]

### 2) Singleness doesn't define your value, ever.

What exactly is "singleness"? I wish we would stop defining things by the absence of something else. Being single doesn't mean you're somehow "incomplete" until someone else completes you. Let's pause to consider that even the idea of singleness is false at its best, and oppression at its worst.

In the first century, Apostle Paul wrote 1 Corinthians 7 specifically to address single people. To paraphrase, he said, "If you want to get married, good. If you want to stay single, good, and it could be better." To you, this might sound ordinary. But at the time, it was a loaded bombshell. This was actually an entirely *revolutionary view of sexuality* that had been previously unheard of.

During Paul's life, the Emperor of the Roman Empire was actually charging a fee for the unmarried because it was considered bad for the economy and the family (never mind that Caesar was already bad for both). Being married with a family was considered the gold status of society, and a single person could only have been a widow or prostitute; there was no middle ground.[34]

So Paul comes along, and moved by the Spirit of God, completely wrecked the whole idea of family and marriage and singles. Though marriage is desirable, it's not a "state of completion," and we have an entire church of brothers and sisters in Christ who are meant for deep soul-community, for both singles and couples. Paul legitimized singleness as an absolutely acceptable life-choice, but more than that, said it can often be better for carrying out God's mission on earth (1 Cor. 7:29-35). Paul himself was single, which itself would've been quite a scandal.

### 3) Please don't allow singleness to rush you into being not-single.

Take as long as it takes. In the same passage (1 Cor. 7), Paul is urging us to *not rush into relationships*. Not only is rushing this unwise because we could shortcut God's growth in our lives, but we could end up getting into a string of bad relationships or making other

---

[34] For more on this, check out Timothy Keller's sermon "Sexuality and Christian Hope," April 18, 2004

poor judgment calls when we're clouded by the impatience to be with someone. Again, *relationships are hard work.* Pursuing anything goes beyond our idealistic hologram picture into a gritty, sweaty, pulsing reality that requires our everything.

God might or might not send someone to you tomorrow: but so long as you're pursuing God, you might hardly notice. That's a good thing. Find Christ, you find yourself, and maybe you'll find someone else.

**4) Your season of un-attached life, or the "gift of singleness," is a unique season like no other.**

There is a very particular way that God works through us when we're not married or attached somehow, and it's downright *impossible* for God to do those things any other way. I'm not trying to diminish one status or the other, but there are pros and cons to both which cannot overlap. I'm about to be married soon, but my married friend tells me the other day, "Use your remaining time wisely. Have a lot of solitude. Take long drives. Read as much as you can. Once you're married, that's it. It's good, but so is your time right now."

**5) It might simply be that others are intimidated by you.**

It could just be that your godliness is thinning out the dating pool. That's a good thing, too.

When I was single and I went after the lady who is my fiancé now, I have to tell you that I was totally intimidated by her. She was godly, she was a strong career woman, and she didn't flirt back easily. Compared to her, I was a scrub, and I knew I couldn't really pursue her unless I got it together. It could be very possible that other men see you as super-awesome, and as with most men, we're just trying to get confident enough to make a move.

**6) It's okay for ladies to give a hint.**

Do you see a dude you like? Ask him out for coffee.

Do you really, really want to meet someone?

It's okay to be in situations where you meet people.

Are you kind of shy or new to the whole thing?

It's okay to ask a friend for help. It's okay to pray together.  ·

**7) Before relational intimacy with others, we first need relational intimacy with God.**

My friend, again: I know this is a very tough time. Anything I've stated here is not a magic formula or silver bullet that will suddenly wash away the nights alone. I don't mean to minimize anything you're feeling, because I do believe most of us are called to be married, and singleness can be a tough time.

So I want to encourage you to continue to seek after God and trust Him. That's probably the predicable pastor-ish thing to say, yet *no one* can give you the validation, affirmation, and approval that God gives you. If we squeeze that from a spouse, we will crush them and crush ourselves. Before we can rightly estimate people in our lives, we must first hold an accurate picture of God and who He is, so that our foundation would be deepened to the very bottom of our roots.

But more than simply seeing God as a vehicle to fill us, He is also the center of all things, the one who in Himself is worthy of all our affection. He is the pure beauty we've been seeking in all our relational ties; He is the only love who knows us exactly as we are, the very depth of our ugliness, yet He continues to pursue us and press in. I know that you know this. Sometimes it feels like a pithy consolation prize, like "Yes I know God is God, but I want a date." I just know that the more I press into Jesus, the more I understand that he became ugly so we might become beautiful, he was single his whole life and calls us his bride, he stayed on a cross to absorb all the ways we have failed: such a costly love puts all others in their place. My situation might hurt me or maim me, and life is never easy, but we have one who stands with us always, who gives me a value and dignity apart from whatever I'm going through or have done, and in this, I am never truly alone. Each day, even with my tiny frail faith, this is enough. Trust Him, bask in Him, know His glory. (You are absolutely loved by Him, as if you were the only one that ever was.)

*"You are significant without a significant other."*[35]
— Shauna Niequist

*"Being single allows the freedom to serve God in ways that a married person may not be able to with their concentration focused on their family. Also, this 'gift' of singleness may only be for a period of time. It should be embraced instead of being a struggle to rush into marriage."*[36]
— Timothy Keller

## 5. About Dating a Non-Christian
### "What are your thoughts on dating a non-Christian?"

My very short answer on a Christian dating a non-Christian is: *Don't do it.*

And it's not even because of "religious differences" or "moral quandaries" or "Can we homeschool the kids?" Committing your heart to another person is already a pretty huge deal, and it's hard enough finding someone who is legit and compatible. If you throw one more complexity into the mix, you're just making it

---

[35] http://www.shaunaniequist.com/significant-without-significant/
[36] Timothy and Kathy Keller, *The Meaning of Marriage* (New York: Riverhead, 2011), p. 247

unnecessarily difficult for yourself — when all along is a much better fit for you who loves Jesus like you do.

We can say something like "love is blind" or "love wants what it wants," which is cute for a little while until you're both running separate paths without hardly understanding each other or knowing why you're driven to live that counter-cultural life.

Finding a decent godly man or a spiritually strong woman is already an uphill task, and two Christians dating have enough problems of their own.

Here's the inconsistency:

*so true*

*How can we overlook something as critical as faith while breaking up over even smaller things like height, man-hands, Hobbit feet, and eyes-too-close-together?*

I'm being silly here, but when most of the culture is quick to break up over pithy non-reasons while condemning those of faith for finding others of the same faith – there is a large gap in logic.

Our faith is not just what we believe, but a *journey of where we are going*. It encompasses our destination, character, empowerment, the narrative we speak over our lives, and everything in between. If someone doesn't get this about you but has a little extra cash in his pocket or a pretty nose, I think we need to do a gut-check on our priorities.

I wouldn't ever say, "Don't date a dude if he's not a Christian." That's not for me to say. What I *would* say is, "Don't date a dude just because he's pretty in the face and can sweet-talk you from your perch and he's got a couple zeros on his bank statement and he has sweaty glistening rock-abs." That's usually what it comes down to.

When we're attracted to a person primarily for shallow-surface reasons, we dismiss the deep spiritual connection that will actually grow the both of you. The spiritual/internal "I-get-you" is really the only meaningful element that will keep you persevering for the long-term.

Just so you know, "I-get-you" doesn't mean he likes the same music or movies or you both can whisper dreamy baby-talk on the phone for hours. "I get you" means ("I get you love Jesus more than anything, and as tough as it is, I'm in on that adventure right with you.") YES

While I have seen the very, very, very rare relationship work out between two spiritually incompatible people, usually one ends up bending to the other, or they have a split life, or the Christian goes numb and accepts the blindness.

And we must consider that if Jesus is who he says he is, then we'd do well to extract ourselves from anyone who actively draws us away from the source of all life. Not to guilt you in any way, but none of us are going to stand before God one day and say, "Well that guy was totally worth it." The biggest struggle I often see is not merely the battle to overcome ourselves, but also when we've fallen into settling for less and selling ourselves short. (Complacency is so much more dangerous than conflict.)

Dear friend: If you're already in a long-term relationship with a non-Christian, I know this isn't going over well. You probably made up your mind and it's not my job to judge you nor persuade you. Maybe you are the very rare exception, and while I don't want to bet on that, perhaps the other person will come around and wake up to Jesus. I pray you do what you can to help your significant-other to Christ while not being wooed away yourself. There's no formula for that either. He or she will either come around, or they won't.

I also don't want you to feel like it's "Too late, I'm stuck." If you're married, then you're pretty much stuck — in a good way, and you best work on that as best you can with the Lord.

Otherwise you have a choice, and as cliché as it sounds, you *do* have the power to pick the God-honoring decision regardless of your past, your baggage, or your history with this relationship. (Please don't ever feel like you're anchored down to something less than what you deserve just because you've invested so much into it.)

Commitments are good, but not if you're speeding down the wrong way of a one-way street.

We get trapped thinking we owe a debt to debt, but for once I'd like to hear someone say, *"Here and no further. I know what's right, and I'm going to quit looking behind me like I owe the past. I owe myself better than this."*

That's not just about relationships. This is about what you're really about. I'm praying for both your discernment and a daily grace for you to wisely traverse this tricky road.

### 6. About "The Right One," aka Soul-Mates

**"Do you think it's possible to know that the person you're with is the person you're going to marry? Even if it's something that wouldn't take place until maybe a few more years, is it possible for us to know that the person we're currently with is the person we're gonna marry? Does God allow us to know that? And if so how would we know? I'm currently battling with trying to understand this better, and if there's anything biblical that may go in line with this & your thoughts on this also!"**

Hey my dear friend, I have two thoughts on this that could make it harder for you to decide, but will hopefully also free you up to make a more informed decision.

1) I absolutely do not believe that "God's Will" is a fixed straight line.

2) I believe that God is more concerned with who you become than what you do. He cares about both, but God primarily sees your heart before your choices.

Whenever someone asks me, "Is the person I'm dating the *one?*" — I always wonder if this is born out of panic or desperation or the anxious urge to be not-single. Because when you suddenly convince yourself that this person *must* be the only person for me: then what happens if this person turns out to be way different than what you've perceived? What if they suddenly leave you? What if they use you up and spit you out? Are we then trapped by "God's Will" to keep going?

I think the idea of God's Will is way more flexible than our self-persuasion, and that it's unwise to enslave ourselves to a singular picture of how things must work out. I don't mean to presume your motives at all, but I wouldn't want you to get imprisoned by this either. Some of us who fall for this "fixed blueprint" for God's Will end up punishing themselves because they think they're now running after Plan B or some lesser version of God's plans.

It's very possible that God *could* point out His plans for you. I wouldn't dismiss that either. Most missionaries feel called, or a pastor gets "the calling," or you feel that God is calling you out of your career into another. But most of the time, God wants you to *be* a certain type of person. This means that a thoughtful decision about your relationship involves understanding the *partnership* and where it will go in fifty years. Any dude off the street can give you a good time for a few weekends, or even a few months. A deeper relationship though is painstakingly carved from marble and plunges to the depths of your guts.

If you're looking for marriage, try to imagine growing old with this person and having your future kids around them. Try to imagine this person on date-night when you're sixty years old. Try to imagine when all your looks are gone and all you have left is your mind and your heart. *Good point. i dig that.*

I can almost guarantee your "one" won't fit your current checklist — though he or she certainly could — not only since God enjoys surprising us, but because every single person is uniquely crafted, wildly complex, and wonderfully flawed. A soul-mate is infinitely more boring than the real whole person we will eventually find.

Once you do feel a certain person is *the one*, then be ready to work on yourself. You'll be tempted to start right at the partnership: but without a hard look at yourself first, you won't even know what to work on, and you'll end up blaming the other person for everything that goes wrong. Without a healthy daily repentance in prayer and Scripture and fellowship, you'll be dang near intolerable when it comes to resolving conflicts or making decisions together. Again: God *does* care about what you do, but He mostly cares about *who you are*. Rest in His grace and run after Him, and you'll find the peace to make those informed decisions.

*In his heart a man plans his course, but the LORD determines his steps.*
— Proverbs 16:9

*If the LORD delights in a man's way, he makes his steps firm;*
*though he stumble, he will not fall, for the LORD upholds him with his hand.*
— Psalm 37:23-24

*Search me, O God, and know my heart; test me and know my anxious thoughts.*
*See if there is any offensive way in me, and lead me in the way everlasting.*
— Psalm 139:23-24

*this verse is so important*

### 7. Starting It Right: A God-Centered Relationship

"Hi, Pastor J! I'd like to say that I've been in good terms with a friend and he recently confessed his feelings for me. I told him that I felt the same way but we agreed not to go steady immediately; instead, develop our friendship first. It's going well so far and we try our best to center God in our relationship. We go online to have Bible study every night, and comfort each other with the Word of God. Just wondering if you have any thoughts on how to make this a more fruitful relationship?"

Hey my friend, here are a few ways to consider for kick-starting you both together.

- Many relationships are built on shallow insubstantial things. Lots of fluff, no substance. *So dig deep on what matters to you and be willing to talk about important heavy issues*, whether it's about spirituality or the church or the human condition or how you see things. Some of this will sound like venting and it could be awkward: but no one is designed for superficial living. God made us to connect to a spiritual reality on a regular basis, and if you're not having profound insightful discussions at least every week, both of you will stagnate. Try it, and you will not only grow, but it'll be more fun than you think.

- Share good books and good sermons together. Use discernment for these too.

- **Pray with the person you're dating.** Find time for God together. Pray with each other (if you're okay with that) or pray for each other in your solitude. It's always a little self-conscious at first, but break through those spiritual hang-ups and share your convictions.

- Know when to say no.  Draw clear boundaries.  Dudes: no always means no, even when it's not spoken out loud.

- Dating will look different for everyone.  There's no "checklist" — because if there were, we instantly become Pharisees who ease our conscience with a mechanical set of rules.

- Please do not ninja-date. Tell your pastor. Get others involved. Get to know each others' parents.

- **Be clear about the future.**  It's not like you're asking for marriage here, but still: be clear that you're not really fooling around.  I mean there's a chance this won't work out, which is not the end of the world, but you don't want to get into this halfheartedly with no plan.

*cute* - **Serve together.**  Anywhere.

- Hang out with old couples to see what they're like.

- **Praise together.**  Those are really the best times ever.

*all of those are so solid wow*

## Chapter 3.5
## Breaking The Creepy Cult Of Beastly Beauty

*Giving A Person More Attention Because They're*
*Attractive: And We All Do It*

Ever prayed more for someone just because they're hot?

Come on, I've done that, too. Let's not act like we're above judging looks here. We give more credibility to someone based on their defined jaw-line and bigger bra size than their less tangible patience and hospitality and compassion.

A very fleshy part of our human nature presumes that good-looking people are also just good, or that less good-looking people don't really count.

In church it's easy to ask for prayer requests from the well-off, well-dressed, clean-cut, easily approachable mid-twenties demographic. Not the weird cat lady off the street, not the dude with the one rotten tooth who talks up a storm, not the pale socially awkward kid who says dorky things.

Most Christian books have the same problem. They're geared to that same easygoing group of believers who attend the same mega-church in a crimeless suburban gated neighborhood with the sparkling 2.5 kids and Hollywood-acceptable appearance, but they have nothing to say for the sick struggling screwed-up former addict who can't find a job because he just "looks wrong."

Wired into all our brains is the deception that appearance means more than it should.

But if I could give you a pair of X-ray goggles, you'll see a bunch of skeletons with the same hopes, dreams, ambitions, anxieties, and worries that everyone else has too.

That seventeen year old pimply kid who loves Call of Duty is the same bag of meat and bones as the athletic football captain with the perfect hair; that girl who everyone hates because of her "overweight" body could just as easily have been the same girl with the slightly higher cheekbones who runs the gang of cheerleaders. You can honk your car horn at the punk teenager on his skateboard crossing the street, but then wave at the old lady on her walker — when both are just people who run deeper than what you see.

Take a Spiritual X-Ray and we all have the same vacuum of eternity within our souls with the same desperate longing inside. You and I could do *way better* than our visual addiction to all things sight, and instead see by *vision*.

We've heard of the famous psychology experiment in which a group of men were given pictures of women they would call over the phone to strike up a friendship.[37] The pictures were not really of the women. In the cases where the woman pictured was less physically attractive (at least by worldly standards), the men would treat her less favorably on the phone. The woman in turn would respond sharply, creating a self-fulfilling prophecy of circular expectations. In the case where the pictured woman was "attractive," the man went all-out in getting to know her. The response was just as eager.

That experiment always makes me a little sick to my stomach because I'm sure I've frequently done the same thing. It's so easy, and even understandable. The world culture hasn't helped in all this. The global market has made a market out of people, instilling an instant reflex of "hot or not" that rips the human out of human beings. There's a lot of money to be made in it.

I grew up most of my school years being called ugly or "rated a zero," and there was always a crushing sense of being treated as a subhuman second-class citizen. When people spoke to me, I could see it in their eyes too. People would talk to me but not really talk to me, their eyes darting for someone else more important in the room.

[37] Snyder, Tanke, and Berscheid, "Journal of Personality and Social Psychology." 1977, Vol. 35. No. 9

There was always a hesitant rush, like people had better places to be than being caught with one of "those" guys.

As stereotypical and harsh as it is, I've found that people who never grow out of the "appearance" phase end up in the garbage dump of history because they relied on their looks to carry them through life, when by the time they're forty, they get the same face as everyone else: wrinkled, worn, and done. It's just age, but many of us don't know how to grow up with dignity. You can only post so many half-naked pictures of yourself on Facebook before your body says no. Some of us never catch on that God cares less about what we do or how we look, but about the *kind of people* we are becoming.

Rather than feel guilty about this whole thing, we can only be empowered to *really get to know each other.* To see beyond physicality and to dive into the fullness of human friendship, to fight the reflex of facial evaluation, to opt for humility instead of sizing-up superiority. None of that is easy because our default mode is judgment, but that little extra work to pull from the gravity of appearance will go a long way to a deeper fulfilled joy in our relationships. I don't want to rob myself of getting to know you simply because of some idiotic postmodern notion that image counts above all. Image never matters where life actually matters.

I imagine Jesus going to the blind, beggars, lepers, sick, demon-possessed, and little children, and I bet he fit right in. Maybe no one could tell it was Jesus from afar, because they expected someone cleaner. I wonder if Jesus bent down on one knee to the girl with the cleft lip, touched her face, and called her beautiful. I wonder if he prayed for her right on the spot, hugged her, pulled back her hair and told her to smile. I wish I could've seen her light up, throw off all insecurity, and do something worthy with her life.

That's what Jesus is about. I want to be about that too,

## The Idolatry Of Youth and Beauty In The Church

You'll know that the Cult of Beauty is happening in your church because —

1) Every promo and insert and church bulletin uses only younger more attractive people.

2) Older people are quarantined to the shelf, which causes them to be demoralized or instantly rejected.

3) Distorted images of "perfect beauty" cause both men and women to have unrealistic expectations, so they pass over great prospects for dating. It's for physical reasons, but no one wants to admit that.

4) No one knows how to age gracefully. We learn how to live well, but no one knows how to *die well.* Older people try to be young and old at the same time, and this is known as *The Idolatry of Youth Culture.*[38] Personally, I really love getting old, but many can't stand it, so it leads to all kinds of immature desperation to stay young. There's always at least one much older praise leader with a chain wallet, frosted tips, skinny jeans, and a fake orange tan. If that's you, God has grace for you too: but let's pray about that one.

5) Physicality becomes morality. In other words, we equate "looking good" with "feeling good" and "being good." This causes all kinds of arrogance and depression.

6) And of course: We pay more attention to attractive people. We pray more for them. We go to them first. We tend to think they're smarter, better behaved, more spiritual, and that they'll somehow increase our social capital.

---

[38] Inspired by Mike Cosper, http://www.thegospelcoalition.org/article/the-idolatry-of-youth-culture-in-worship/

[39]"14 Ways To Handle A Christian Introvert," http://jsparkblog.com/2012/12/13/14-ways-to-handle-a-christian-introvert/ and
http://jspark3000.tumblr.com/post/37804515166/14-ways-to-handle-a-christian-introvert

Just as with the bias against introverts,[39] there is an even wider systemic prejudice against "less attractive" people, and the church doesn't do much better than the world does. Pastors still make fat-jokes, race-jokes, female-jokes, or do the stuttering voice for Moses or the effeminate voice for Jacob. And I can't say I've always steered clear of these pitfalls either. Our culture is so drenched in insensitivity, we tend to belittle others without even noticing.

It's no wonder that even within the church, we have extreme issues with body image, and consequently, self-harm and self-loathing. If we don't meet a certain physical standard, we're often pushed out of an "inner-circle," and these invisible walls are much thicker than cliques or class. It's simply not talked about in church, because no one wants to think we're so ugly inside to reject people based on appearance. We each want to assume we're fair and accepting, but the longer we deny our biases, the more it will control us and the attitude in our churches, our jobs, and our homes.

If you've been a victim of this, the only way to break these barriers is for *you to speak up first, but speak graciously*. Be open, honest, real, and loving. **Reach out persistently and patiently until you are heard**. Have grace for others' lack of grace. I know that sounds unfair. And if your pastor or church or fellow comrades in Christ continually cut you out after you've been open with them, then consider another community. But stewing in bitterness over rejection will only make things worse. People like you and I have an uphill battle (I'm an Asian-American in a predominantly non-Asian culture, and not so attractive), but it's no excuse to act out when we're alienated. A poor attitude is ugly no matter who it's coming from.

But more than that: In our rejection, we can remember the Gospel. That sounds like a Christianese thing to say, but Jesus was a plainly unattractive man who ultimately became the ugliest one of us all (Isaiah 53:2-3). On the cross, he hung naked and humiliated (Matthew 27:35). God, the most beautiful being in the universe, became an impoverished destitute man of sorrows, so that we might become rich in beauty (2 Corinthians 8:9).

This is *not* a consolation prize, but it is the all-encompassing treasure and purpose and glory of our lives. None of us can truly attain a perfect beauty on our own no matter how much we try, but Jesus, who was truly beautiful, became ugly so that we might gain the perfect beauty. What we could never achieve in ourselves, Jesus bestowed for us as a pure gift without conditions.

When you can know this, then while physical rejection certainly still hurts, it will only be a smaller symptom of a broken world that just doesn't understand true value. We can have grace for that. We can find security in Christ first, and then go into the world to display our heart's true splendor.

And for those who are stuck in the Cult of Beauty — you can remind yourself that the cross of Christ flipped our worldly values upside-down. True authority is humility. True glory is sacrifice. And true beauty begins on the inside, where Christ resides.

All this sounds very ideal, I know. It will never be easy. But please do not seek validation from your pastor, or your friends, or your culture, or magazines and music and ads and movies. These will all come up short, as you already know they are. Rest in Christ's love, and then you will have a confident grace for others even when they reject you, whether it's over your looks or your speech or your personality or you. Rejection will come and go, but God's love is our permanent constancy.

*God changes hearts yall*

"*The worldly man treats certain people kindly because he 'likes' them: the Christian, trying to treat every one kindly, finds him liking more and more people as he goes on — including people he could not even have imagined himself liking at the beginning.*"[40]
— C.S. Lewis

'*The LORD does not look at the things man looks at. Man looks at the outward appearance, but the LORD looks at the heart.*"
— 1 Samuel 16:7b

"*Your beauty should not come from outward adornment, such as braided hair and the wearing of gold jewelry and fine clothes. Instead, it should be that of your inner self, the unfading beauty of a gentle and quiet spirit, which is of great worth in God's sight.*"
— 1 Peter 3:3-4

## Why I Didn't Record My Marriage Proposal

A symptom of all this beauty-idolatry is the compulsive urge to post our best moments on social media. Every life in public looks like they're having the time of their lives. We're steeped in a scrolling feed of comparison and competition.

I do love our culture of display. I love that we can share our deepest most personal moments in a one-click treasure trove.

Seriously. I'm not a cranky old dude who hates the new wave of technology.

But I didn't want to record my own marriage proposal.

I'm not against this at all. It doesn't make me better than anyone else. But as for me, I just want to keep it in here, between me and my wonderful lady, and not for the world to see.

---

[40] C.S. Lewis, *Mere Christianity* (New York: HarperCollins, 1952, 1980), p. 132

There's something about recording an event that feels alarmingly self-conscious. It's sort of a heightened hyper-reality, like I'm thinking ahead to how it'll be seen, like I'm not really *there* but stuck in a superimposed future.

There's something about squeezing a memory into YouTube that feels driven by a performer's paranoia, like I must get every moment just right to get the maximum views, the most tears, the most thumbs up.

I don't mean to sound old-fashioned. Really.

But I'm one of those guys who loves the power of story. The simplicity of re-telling, with my hands and my eyes and my voice, in a chair right in front of you, looking far off to remember every pulsing moment. The quiver in my lips. The smile I can hardly contain. That final breath after the final word.

**It is the sharing of our human experience by human means that allows the seed of imagination to bloom.** Of course videos can do that. But videos cannot exercise the paintbrush of our spirit. It does the painting for us. Sometimes that is good, but it demands nothing. It's not *involved*. A video is occasionally like walking through a museum. A story invites you in to participate, to ride on a journey in that invisible space between your head and your heart.

When my future wife or I pass away, and if God allows us the grace to be with each other on our last days, then we won't have a video of the day I proposed. Maybe it will be a loss. But we will have our laughter. We will have our tears. We will have an ocean of memory running deep in our veins, a rushing river of intimacy that no one can invade. We can remember together. It will be our private moment. It will be the last thought on my deathbed, and so as I go, it will go as well.

The world can't have that one.
It belongs to me, to her, and to God.

*memories are to be cherished*

## *The Just-Because Love*

When I was about seven years old, my family owned a martial arts dojo and one of our students was a model. She was a tall beautiful blonde lady who was practically family, and she invited everyone to her very first Beauty Pageant.

I remember being in the back room where the ladies prepared for the walkway. There were tons of mirrors and harsh lights and ladies fitting into impossible clothing. I was too young to understand all these things, but a part of me wanted to tell these ladies that they didn't have to do this. They didn't need to compete against each other. Trophies for everyone, why not?

My family and I sat in the front row. We cheered when our amazing blonde student took the stage. But — she didn't really look like herself. I was used to seeing her in class, hair flying and kicking the bag and throwing men over her shoulder. I have nothing (much) against Beauty Pageants, but this wasn't our friend.

Three older men in suits were judging all the contestants with scores down to the decimal. I was a kid, but I wanted to rip those scorecards out of their hands and rip off their fancy neckties.

Our lady didn't win. She got a Runner-Up prize. She had to smile the whole time while three other ladies got these huge medals and scholarships.

In the back room again, she was crying her eyes out. Mascara carved valleys in her face. Someone told her, "Runner-Up's not bad." I couldn't wrap my head around the fact that someone even had to make such a statement.

The one clear thing I remember that night is walking up to my friend as she wept in her chair, and we were face-to-face, and I whispered in her ear, *"Jeanie ... They were wrong."*

They were dead-wrong.

She broke a smile through those dark runny tears.

I never forgot it.

I think about how easily we confuse the traits of a person with the whole person, how we latch onto physicality when those things go with time.

Whenever you love somebody, there's usually a list. "I love you because of ___." Your voice. Your hair. Your confidence. The way you crinkle your nose when you laugh. How you change your mind a hundred times at the drive-thru. How you bend down to a child to speak to them at eye level. How you look in a mean dress.

But at the bottom of this long list, God always adds one more. He says, "I love you just-because." No specific reason, not based on externals, and not even based on anything we say or do. It just is. Because we all get old and gray. We all change over a lifetime. The reasons that others love us never stay the same, because we are a people in progress shaped by the edges of time. God loves us when our souls turn ugly, when we are cowardly and crass, when we fail and stumble, when we lose patience at the drive-thru and set a poor example for children. He loves us when the dress stops fitting. He loves us when those who've seen our underbelly silently walk away. Our God is the God who stays when everyone else leaves.

And when our voice fades, when our hair is gone, when we can hardly laugh without pain: God loves us just because. He can't help it. This is who He is, regardless of who we are, because His love does not reside in a list. His love is free. It is reckless. It is forever.

*"I have loved you with an everlasting love."*
— *Jeremiah 31:3*

what a beautiful gift.

*"... Jesus knew that the hour had come for him to leave this world and go to the Father. Having loved his own who were in the world, he loved them to the end."*
— *John 13:1*

His love for us is so real

# Chapter 4
# Heartbreak, Break-Ups, Crushes, and Navigating The Wreckage

## *That Time I Tried To Kill Myself Over A Girl*

I'm going to jump in the deep end here.

Just ten years ago, I tried to kill myself over a girl. She had cheated on me twice so I swallowed a bottle of pills and waited for her to find me dead. Part of me wanted to win her back and the other part of me wanted to end it all. Neither worked.

Looking back, I feel a sad sort of amusement about the whole thing. To this day, I still struggle with depression and that's some very serious business, but to actually have tried to kill myself over *another person* makes me a bit embarrassed. Sometimes it garners sympathy and affirming looks, but other times I see people back away with incredulity, as if they would never let themselves take their drama so far.

Yet I want to tell the ones who don't understand: *It's so very easy to get attached to a person, an idea, a "dream," a type of future, and then get sick to your stomach over every part of it until you want to die.*

It can happen to anyone. Drugs are not the only addictive substance. There's this overwhelming soul-withering sickness for people like me who quickly latch onto a person and feed off their being. We wait for their call and examine their every move and flinch at their every word and hang on their every breath.

It sounds awful, because it is. It's a panicked desperation to overly cater to another person's every whim — and until you've been there, you have no clue how low a human being can go to feed the codependency. It takes so much effort and energy and inhuman strength to remove this horrible addiction from our blood, because it's been so ingrained into us from years of abuse and abandonment and rejection. You can't know how bad it gets until you're the one sprawled out on the cold tile floor with an empty bottle of pills in your lifeless hand.

Everyone has their own idea of the future, and at any moment it can be smashed to pieces. We're not in as much control of our lives as we tend to think. And [the more you plant your hope into **something so untenable, so will your soul dry up into a soul that is collapsible.**]

My dream was to be with this woman, and my nightmare was her leaving me. But — this made me controlling, manipulative, angry, selfish, neurotic. And in a sense, I drove her into the arms of other men. It doesn't make it right, but it does explain it. It was just as much her decision as it was mine. And by the time I swallowed the bottle of Excedrin, I was already dead inside. I was just discarding the husk that once contained the person I used to be.

I am begging you now: *If you're in this place of over-attachment to anything outside of you, please find a healthy way to handle it or just leave.* Otherwise you will crush that person, that dream, that future, and you will be crushed by it too. Nothing can be sustained under the weight of your idolatrous expectations, including you. It'll be worth your time to seek counseling, seek outlets, seek real help — and don't get addicted to the recovery either. You need to learn to be alone with the silent vacuum of your own thoughts: because when you honestly confront the ugliness inside, you will be liberated from the weight of yourself.

And if you've recently been walking in the shattered remnants of an old dream and you just want to end it all — *please, please, please believe me that there is always yet hope on the other side.* I know what it feels like right now. I know that all the colors have been smothered by a gray heavy fog, that your hollowed out stomach feels like someone is punching you in the gut from inside. I know it's hard to wake up, hard to sleep, hard to breathe, that you'd rather die than feel this way. I know. It will feel this way for a while. And I can't connect the dots on what life is supposed to "teach" you, because lectures don't heal anything.

But I am pleading with you to take the next painful step forward, because your life is more precious than what has happened. I'm pleading with you to consider **that there are other dreams, that life is flexible, that people can start over every day**. I hope you will do all it takes to wake up tomorrow with even just the simple goal of breathing, because you're an important part of this human narrative even when it's just to breathe. And as the pain leaves, as it always does, I hope you do not refuse the comfort of good friends and the counsel of wise people and the offer of ice cream and hot coffee and a midnight conversation where you might crack a smile again for the first time in a long time as you reconstruct your pieces for something better. All this is worth making it through today.

I'm not writing this from a wrapped-up bowtie of a life. I'm still fractured in so many places of the soul; I still feel depression sinking its bony fingers into my sides. But I've also found that in the healing, by the grace of God and through wonderful friends, that life is worth living. If you think it hurts right now — **healing hurts even more, because you have to get up and move.** But I'd rather hurt this way. If life has to be pain, then I'd rather hurt moving forward than sitting down.

I can't tell you that it "gets better," because the last ten years were still tough. I can't tell you that ever since near-death, that I've been all *carpe diem*. I can't even tell you that I learned all these important life-lessons, because I don't believe pain needs to be allegorized.

But I can tell you that I should've been dead ten years ago in that sterile lonely hospital bed — and I'm so very glad I'm still alive.

I can tell you that I let go of dreaming a single dream, because no one is meant to limit their imagination to a singular shaky ideal. Even though life is pain and it can knock the wind right out of you, it can also take your breath away. And I've learned that when you're at the end of yourself and when everything else has slipped away: all we really have is God, and He is enough. I'm asking you to consider there is a God who is not distant from your hurt but really loves you through it all, and as much as you hate to hear this, He's just as hurt about this as you are. You might have heard that a million times and we might acknowledge it in our heads: but it's only in the deepest abyss where we find God is deeper still, and He's the only true stable anchor. It's only in such exquisite pain that God really makes sense. It's there that only God can help you.

**You can get over what's over, because you're not over yet.** I hope you choose to live. I hope you put the blade away. I hope you delay until the morning. I hope you talk it out. I hope you can look back in ten years and grieve over your old dreams with a quiet laughter. I hope you keep hoping.

"*Friends, why are you doing this? We too are only human, like you. We are bringing you good news, telling you to turn from these worthless things to the living God, who made the heavens and the earth and the sea and everything in them.*"
— Acts 14:15

"*Every good thing we could think or desire is to be found in this same Jesus Christ alone. For, He was sold, to buy us back; captive, to deliver us; condemned, to absolve us; He was made a curse for our blessing, sin offering for our righteousness; marred that we may be made fair; he died for our life; so that by Him fury is made gentle, wrath appeased, darkness turned into light, fear reassured, despisal despised, debt canceled, labor lightened, sadness made merry, misfortune made fortunate, difficulty easy, disorder ordered, division united, ignominy ennobled, rebellion subjected, intimidation intimidated, ambush uncovered, assaults assailed, force forced back, combat combated, war warred against, vengeance avenged, torment tormented, damnation damned, the abyss sunk into the abyss, hell transfixed, death dead, mortality made immortal. In short, mercy has swallowed up all misery, and goodness all misfortune. For all these things which were to be weapons of the devil in his battle against us, and the sting of death to pierce us, are turned for us into exercises which we can turn to our profit. If we are able to boast with the Apostle, saying, O hell, where is thy victory? O death, where is thy sting? It is because by the Spirit of Christ, we live no longer, but Christ lives in us.*"[41]
— John Calvin

---

[41] From the preface of a French translation of the New Testament, by Pierre Robert Olivétan

## *You Can Quit Punishing Yourself,*
## *And The Grace of God Revokes That Too*

This might not be your story today, but relational regret is bound to happen and I want us to be ready. Some of us will be deceived. Or betrayed. Or manipulated. Used. Abused. And we often blame ourselves. It will cause us to believe a False Narrative over our lives, a rehearsed inner-loop of anger at ourselves, and some of us know that it's downright debilitating.

My friend: If you're living through the consequences of your actions or the actions of others, you have suffered enough. You don't have to pay it off through your guilt. You can quit beating yourself up about what you've done or what's been done to you. You don't have to settle for coping with your losses or crawling back to zero.

Grace has you covered.

There's a term called "time served" in which an imprisoned defendant is let go after the trial. He or she has already served time in jail during the trial. Most lawyers would call this a win because there's no extended prison sentence.

Your consequences is your *time served.* You have spent dozens of hours in regret, cleaning up your mess, navigating the broken pieces, unable to reclaim what was lost, trying to fix what remains.

But the devil gets you thinking **you have to pay more to compensate for your wrongs**. So we add layers of guilt and self-punishment to appear repentant, and maybe your neighbors and your church and your family will *really* see that you're sincere. Maybe if you sit in the back of worship service with your head down and your hands wringing and your shoulders slumped, people will see you're really sorry.

Please don't do this to yourself.

Jesus came to die for this, too.

He has served *all* your time, more than you could know.

Even before you sinned,
while you were planning the sin in your head,
while you were actually sinning,
and afterward when you felt zero regret and had zero intention to change —

*Jesus still absolutely loved you in your mess as He watched you from his prison on the cross.*

Even as you slowly awake to the horror of what you have done — **God sent His Son to die for that very guilt too.** His love preempted your guilt, and Jesus who was free in Heaven became a prisoner on the earth to break you free of your chains.

*Jesus took away the guilt we would feel when we'd realize how he was beaten to a bloody pulp under a Roman's serrated whip and how he bled out through his hands and feet — for you and for me.*

He stood in our place of punishment, but more than that, he even removed the feeling that we deserved it. This is, at least in part, what it means to have our guilt removed, for him to have substituted for us, to have taken on our sin.

We can be free from guilt and move forward in His grace.

Please do not hold yourself back from this joy.

Please do not think your past or your record gets to say who you can be today.

If you must look back, look to learn and to laugh.

Look forward now, as God is making you new.

*"Away with tears and fears and troubles! United in wedlock with the eternal Godhead Itself, our nature ascends into the Heaven of Heavens. So it would be impious to call ourselves 'miserable'. On the contrary, <u>Man is a creature whom the Angels—were they capable of envy—would envy</u>. <u>Let us lift up our hearts!</u>"[42]*

— C.S. Lewis


*For the grace of God that brings salvation has appeared to all men.*

*It teaches us to say "No" to ungodliness and worldly passions, and to live self-controlled, upright and godly lives in this present age, while we wait for the blessed hope—the glorious appearing of our great God and Savior, Jesus Christ, who gave himself for us to redeem us from all wickedness and to purify for himself a people that are his very own, eager to do what is good.*

*These, then, are the things you should teach. Encourage and rebuke with all authority. Do not let anyone despise you.*

— Titus 2:11-15


*At one time we too were foolish, disobedient, deceived and enslaved by all kinds of passions and pleasures. We lived in malice and envy, being hated and hating one another.*

*But when the kindness and love of God our Savior appeared, <u>he saved us</u>, not because of righteous things we had done, but <u>because of his mercy</u>.*

*He saved us through the washing of rebirth and renewal by the Holy Spirit, whom he poured out on us generously through Jesus Christ our Savior, so that, having been justified by his grace, we might become heirs having the hope of eternal life.*

— Titus 3:3-7

---

[42] C.S. Lewis, *The Collected Letters, Vol. 2* (New York: HarperCollins, 2004)

## *Roll Up Your Sleeves: There's Work To Do, And It's You*

There are at least a few of us who believe grace is a Get-Out-Of-Jail-Free Card, and we think, "That's exactly why I'm in trouble in the first place, because I kept saying God would forgive me anyway." Or it's not so much about what's been done to you, but what you've done to others, and you're disturbed by some of the horrible ways you've cheated and tempted and lied to other people. So we think, "There's no way I could just receive grace on that one. Ask my ex-girlfriend, she'll tell you how I really am."

I know the remorse here. I know what it's like to look behind me at a trail of used-up people, wondering why I couldn't stop myself, and feeling like "God-loves-me" was a hollow platitude. I know what it's like to have multiple women in the same town just hate my guts.

If all this grace-talk sounds like it lets you do what you want, I'll counter that by saying *the Grace of God is the only force that could both restore you from your wreckage and empower you to do everything that God wants and envisions and dreams for you.* YES.

Here's where we find that the *love of God is a relentless, reckless, furious, consuming force* that will find us where we are, but will never ever leave us where it found us.

In the Bible, I mostly see that God's law is black and white. "Don't be like this guy" or "The angel of death will slay you" or "Don't do that or things will mushroom-cloud real fast." There are clear-cut lines, sharp boundaries, no wiggle room. The law is iron and oak and all closed fists.

But then everyone in the Bible keeps making these enormous ridiculous mistakes, not just brushing up against the law, but leaping over it full speed. There's a candid sort of rawness with how each story tells the unabashed account of total failure. They purposefully screw up their lives in a near-parody of a reality show. I wouldn't include any of these guys if I was making up a religion.

Your favorite Bible heroes make really good celebrity mug-shots.

And this is where God comes in, every time, first with an arm of discipline and a face-melting intervention — but also with a gentle scooping hand of compassion and a heart of constant mercy. God never lets up on the law, but *He often pays for it Himself by absorbing the cost of what we did.* It's this sort of grace that eventually re-shapes these men and women into thankful people, who can't believe the second chance they've been given, and when the grace kicks in, they never stop getting overwhelmed by Him. They would follow Him anywhere, with zero limits, which is exactly how much grace God shows *us*.

It would've hurt if God had just slapped us around with His divine law. But it *hurts even more* that God steps in with His kindness. It's the type of hurt that tenderizes a heart and revokes our selfishness, because we know God ultimately paid the law with the life of His Son. Where we stood guilty and embarrassed and downright wrong, Jesus loved us up to a cross. There he took upon the consequences of the very law which was meant for our good. To receive grace, it only costs our pride; for God to give grace, the cost was His Son.

His grace is the kind of love that *hurts,* and so then, it is real love.

It's hard to see Jesus there and then go back to who I was. He died to set us wretched ones free. He rose for my new life, that I would see the law as the vision of who I'm to become, not as a measure for how I've failed, but as a future memory of the person I'm meant to be. Only grace will get me there. Only grace can bring me to follow the law with joy, with gratitude, with peace. Only grace can tell me I am both fully flawed and wholly beloved.

On one end, guilt-fear-and-shame are lazy preacher tactics that cripple us into fear-based faith, which isn't sustainable. Guilt has me staring at *me*. But on the other end, half a grace has me staring right through God.

*Only grace can tell me I am both fully flawed & wholly beloved.*

I don't want half a grace.

Half-a-gospel offers a "better life" but neglects our struggle against the devil and the dark — a discount flea market God like a doting grandfather who hand-waves your hurt. It leaves out spiritual warfare, deception, temptation, and prideful rebellion: all the things that hurt you.

***We are in constant battle, and grace is just as much our haven of rest as it is our resolve to fight.***

Faith is a process, yes — but it's in the process where the grace invades, for continued diligence and vigilance to persevere.

Grace will set you free to an empowered, fruitful, passionate, fully forgiven life. It's *not* to enable your affair, our lack of care for the poor, our aversion to serving, or our self-reliance. Please don't mistake grace for enabling, entitlement, or halfway hearts.

**Jesus sets you free for** *a wild, dangerous, painful journey that is not safe nor sterile — but it is joyful and good.*


## *That Icky Awful Unseemly Word "Surrender"*

Really, all this comes down to that awful word **surrender**.

I hated the word "surrender" for so long. It was Super-über Christianese. I ran from it, because I liked my flings, my fantasies, my stash, the dark room, the secrecy, the selection. I wanted to love God and I knew He was good, but *surrender* felt like something only those "radical Christians" do.

To my horror, it's what *every* Christian is called to do.

For everyone who says grace helps us "relax," I get what this means. We don't want a fear-based, guilt-driven, self-righteous kind of faith, so we need God's soul-nurturing love to motivate us into joyful obedience.

But really: **There are some things I don't want to be slack about**. I don't trust my own body to just act on grace all the time.

There are moments
when I must fight for a missional other-centered love,
to sacrifice my own comfort to pour out generosity for my fellow human beings,
to claw after true purity and integrity and humility,
to seek my blind spots with accountability and rebuke,
to flee from destructive desires,
to uppercut my pride and my selfishness,
to seek that elusive God-centered focus called holiness.

Is that legalism? Or can we just stop accusing passionate Christians from our own insecurity?

When I know Jesus, I know love — but love does not pamper. It prunes and perfects and pursues. **It is a sweet embrace *and* a sanctifying chisel.**

I eventually had to confront myself. *Can I really surrender this? To submit? Not just my "lust" and porn and physicality, but every area of my life that really matters? Can I do the scary work that God has called me to do?*

As Tim Keller says, *"It's hard to obey God. But it's harder not to."*

I was between two ends of a widening chasm and being torn in half, and I had to choose. The cognitive dissonance of hypocrisy was slamming on my door. I had to answer for it. So will you.

But soon we learn a wonderful truth, that when you surrender to Him, this is not a restriction or removal or religion. God made us and He knows what's best for us. His Word offers us life. We are essentially trading up towards Him, and we get *Him*.

**When we follow God, anything that first feels like sacrifice is actually giving up what we never needed anyway.** We give up pride, greed, anger, jealousy, and lust — things we find so comforting and familiar but actually kill us — and we get love, peace, joy, wholeness, and His Spirit in return. He wants to flex His Spirit in you to make supernatural fruits for His glory. This is a pretty good deal.

I know this faith-journey will always be a huge battle. We will wrestle in faith all the way to glory. We won't get it right a lot of the time, and any act of righteousness will be a miracle. We'll definitely face some consequences for the things that we've wrought, because a loving God has to let this play out that we might see the hurt we've caused. So then, this must have us wanting more grace, and not less. It must leave us desperate for more of God's surgical love, and not pampering. It must keep us anchored to Him, however imperfectly.

We will sometimes fail. It's okay. But let's not deceive ourselves to settle for less. We get up, we go again.

*But he was pierced for our transgressions,*
*he was crushed for our iniquities;*
*the punishment that brought us peace was on him,*
*and by his wounds we are healed.*
— Isaiah 53:5

*"The prophet [Isaiah] said of God, 'You have put all my sins behind your back.' When something is behind our back, it is out of sight. We can't see it anymore. God says He has done that with our sins. It is not that we haven't sinned or, as Christians, do not continue to sin. We know we sin daily — in fact, many times a day. Even as Christians our best efforts are still marred with imperfect performance and impure motives. But God no longer 'sees' either our deliberate disobedience or our marred performances. Instead He 'sees' the righteousness of Christ, which He has already imputed to us.*

*"Does this mean God ignores our sins like an overindulgent, permissive father who lets his children grow up undisciplined and ill-behaved? Not at all. In His relationship to us as our Heavenly Father, God does deal with our sins, but only in such a way as for our good. He does not deal with us as our sins deserve, which would be punishment, but as His grace provides, which is for our good."[43]*
— Jerry Bridges

---

[43] Jerry Bridges, *Transforming Grace* (Colorado: NavPress, 2008) p. 45

The following seven questions are about the deeper challenges we experience as we go about dating and relationships. Again, please feel free to skip around, and may you be blessed as you find Him by His pursuit of you.

### 1. To Love Without Idolizing A Relationship

**"How do you love someone without idolizing the relationship? I have a tendency to idolize my past relationships, and I'm so afraid of messing up again this time. It makes me almost want to not be with anyone because I know my heart will always default to idolatry. How do other people function and enjoy God's blessings without turning them into idols? I know I should operate out of love, not fear, but fear is driving my decisions now. I'm so afraid of the past repeating itself and I don't trust me."**

My very dear wonderful friend: I had the *very same exact* issue, and in many ways, I'm still inclined to idolize relationships as my entire source of approval, attention, value, and validation. I have a tendency to get "addicted" to things and to squeeze the life out of them, and it's a lifelong problem. I'm sure many others will also tell you they feel the same way; you're not alone on this one.

Your instinct to say *"I don't trust me"* is actually right on. I commend you for this, because there are way too many of us who do what we want and call it "freedom." There are too many philosophies that say "Follow your heart" and "Go be yourself" and "Do what you feel" without any context for reality, and people get stomped. So you're not far from the truth — our hearts are certainly prone to wander.

Yet God doesn't want you to live in fear of "possible idolatry." Then you can just as quickly idolize anti-idolatry, and that will harm you too. If you're worried about messing it up all the time, you'll end up trying to control your flesh with your flesh, which simply leads to other problems. It's just **sin-replacement**, which you already know is not working. By trying so hard not to mess it up, you'll simply mess it up somewhere else. We easily over-think ourselves into unlikely death-trap scenarios, which never actually frees us. We are officially done with that fear.

So here are some suggestions for you.

**1) If you conclude that you can't handle a relationship right now,** *then take a very long extended break from the whole dating scene.*

You can start over. You can flush all those addictive tendencies out of your system. You can take a long, long break from the entire dating scene. I know this sounds like legalism, but please trust me: you will thank me later on this one, even if three weeks from now you meet the hottest Christian ever. In your current state, it wouldn't be wise, and you'll end up ruining both of you.

There are a few of us who *need* the gift of singleness to invest for our future, so it'll be like fasting for a good long season. You'll be able to get your mind right.

That also means possibly quitting the half-flirtations, the late-night texting, the collection of Snapchat buddies, your Instagram follows with all the suggestive pictures, and any possible source of chemistry. Don't turn your opposite-gender friends into possible dating candidates. Quit dragging them through the attraction-evaluation in your brain. You need a time-out to **regain perspective** and remember who you are in Christ.

**2) Just be friends.**

I know you're human and you'll catch some feelings here and there, but it's *up to you* with how you act on them.

As I've said already, a guy and a girl *can* be friends, if we can quit thinking that every person you meet is a romantic possibility.

A lot of this random "crushing" is from our culture of "What can you do for me?" — which leads to objectification and dehumanization. I know that sounds pretentious, but even objectifying an idea of romance or some ideal mystery-dude is still using someone for what they can do. That tingle-twitch you get from flirting is really just an ego-boost because we like it when someone might like us back. On a long enough timeline, it leads to others getting hurt or becoming self-marketing meat on display.

Friendship is the only way to cure that predicament. When you're in the art of being friends with the opposite gender, you'll find a love for them that doesn't regard their physical appearance or "dating material" level. It only regards them for *who they are*. This is tough to do, but if you can hang out in groups and protect your friends' dignity, your mind gets rewired to enjoy them *for them*. It's how God loves us and how we're called to love others.

### 3) Quit listening to everyone else, including me, and think it all the way through.

I sense a tension in you where you want to do what's right — "I know I should operate out of love, not fear" — but this is causing you even more anxiety.

Ultimately this is an ongoing conversation between you and God. That's all Romans 14. While others will have good things to say, when it comes to dating they can just confuse you, and I have a feeling some of this might be the source of your fear.

Everyone from your pastor to super-bloggers to your roommates to the local Christian bookstore is pressuring you into a decision. Even those cool Christian bloggers are telling you to "relax" and just go date. I think some of this advice is good stuff. But some of these voices — *not you* — are paralyzing you with an unnecessary fear that you're somehow doing this wrong. It's hard to know where to step when everyone is yelling at you to watch out, and it feels like you're paying some kind of penalty for not listening to others.

You did confess that you have an idolatry problem, and that's a good first step. Yet you might be freaking yourself out even more. Maybe your fear of idolatry has pushed you to an extreme, or even worse, someone said "you should-should-should" and that choked you with more anxiety.

All that to say, no one has the right to shame you into dating nor scare you out of it either. ***It is your sole decision under God*** and it is *your process* to work through with Him, so don't let my word or anyone else's be the final word. Step back from it all and think hard about this. You don't have to listen to a word I've written here. Pray about it as if you've never heard a single thing about dating, and remember: you are different than anyone else. God has a word for you.

**4) If you get with God on this one, you will confront the honest raw truth about yourself and then find healing.**

Get honest with Him. Over time, you'll know why you idolize relationships. You'll be able to trace it back to your parents' broken home, or some past abusive partner, or a need to people-please, or a fear of being alone.

When you can figure out all the insides of what's going on: you can begin healing in all those areas of your life you might have ignored or only skimmed over. You can make the right godly decisions. You can have God take over and He alone will tell you when you're ready. He has grace for your past and for your future too. He alone will love you into a whole heart so that your relationship will always take a second place to Him — which is exactly as it's meant to be.

This is a messy imperfect process, but it can begin today, now. Don't delay it.

## 5) Get on your God-given adventure.

Find the calling God has for you. When you begin giving your life away within the specific blueprint that God has wired you for — you will slowly be able to love without expecting anything back. You'll be able to remove your desperate tendrils that suck the life out of others.

A lot of times, **idolatry is about expectations.** We try to squeeze from both people and things what only God can give us. But when they don't deliver, we tend to crush the idol, crush ourselves, and become controlled and controlling. The way to break free of idolatry is not to not-sin, but to **walk into the purposes of God with full abandon.**

If you are becoming who God has made you to be and giving your life for His glory — then you automatically enter into the habit of love without expectation and forgiving without retaliation. You become less attached to an idea and begin to appreciate things more *for their essence in itself.* When your sleeves are rolled up in the mess of broken people who can do nothing for you, you will experience a kind of selflessness that makes self-centered living look like a joke — and you won't want to go back.

Find your calling in Christ. It doesn't mean the idolizing tendencies will disappear. But it does mean that when God is your active priority — both in your heart *and* your hands — you will have an appropriate measure for the blessings in your life. Then along the way, as you live your God-made adventure, you'll find someone alongside you running to Him too.

*"Codependency isn't sexy. It isn't romantic. It's built with a fuse and will surely burn out. The healthiest thing you can say to the one you love is, 'I would be okay without you, and that's why I choose to stay.'"[44]*

— Lauren Britt

---

[44] http://yesdarlingido.tumblr.com/post/93614942540/codependency-isnt-sexy

## 2. Getting Over A Break-Up

**"I can't get over the breakup I recently went through with a boy I really love. I've tried so hard to rely on God to get me through, but I'm still hurting so much. I feel guilty that leaning on God for help hasn't been enough to stop hurting."**

I'm really sorry this is happening and I totally feel your pain on this one. I've had seven ex-girlfriends and every break-up totally sucked.

But please, please, please do *not* feel bad about feeling bad. You are allowed to feel your feelings and you're allowed to mourn your loss. You don't have to feel guilty for how you feel. No one including yourself should ever belittle you on what you're going through.

Please do not beat yourself up over this. Weeping over an ex-boyfriend is not idolatry. This is all a natural part of the process called life. Healing takes time and intentionality, but you can go at your own pace.

**A break-up will be a lot like grieving over a death.**[45] You're burying your former schedule, memories, and presence of this other person. That takes time. Wrestle with it each day, not denying the pain or numbing the emotions, but letting it froth to the surface. Some days you'll cry. Some days you'll be angry. But I promise you, it will get easier each day as you bring it to God and move on.

Right now it feels like this is *always* how it will feel like. You'll be tempted to get a rebound or get drunk or to kick your ex in the crotch. Some of us (like me) go into long self-evaluating spirals of loathing. Hang in there. Take these things to the Lord in prayer, and I'll add, you don't have to be pretty about it. Rage out and shake a fist and heave as much as you need.

---

[45] This idea came from Glen Fitzjerrell, popular blogger.

Before you know it, you'll notice all the colors of the world around you again. Food will taste good. You'll find yourself laughing, even about your ex. The empty ache will become dull and you'll feel lighter and you'll be refreshed with God and it'll be like you're meeting Him all over again.

Life goes on, and so must you, and God still has a purpose for you on this earth while you have breath left to live. **Let it hurt, but keep moving.**

In the meantime, hang with your church and your girls and your parents. Talk with your pastor. As much as you're allowed to hurt, also give yourself permission to *have a good time*. Read good books. Be with groups. Try new things. You're also a free person now, so in due time, you'll find a good-looking dude who is chasing Jesus. Be ready to have your past-baggage unloaded before you go there.

I'm rooting for you, and so is God.

### 3. My Crush Went For Someone Else and I'm Devastated

"I recently found out that a church brother I'm crushing on has been interested in another sister for a while. They're committed to each other but also keeping distance to see how things go. I'd be lying if I said I'm alright. I'm absolutely overwhelmed with anger, sorrow, self-pity and jealousy all bubbling at the core of my being. It is so utterly difficult for me to put God first and not look for approval from men. How do I move forward and learn to find my identity and security in God alone?"

Hey my friend, the best thing is to let all those emotions wash out of your system each day as you let it go, and vent as much as you like to your closest friends and to God Himself. He can certainly handle it.

However, I have to be very, very blunt with you here, because I love you and I want you to be better. Please hear this as balanced wisdom, and that I both sympathize with your pain and want to offer a bit of sober reality.

It's possible this is the best thing that could've ever happened to you. I don't mean that in a positive way like "God has another plan" or "Just wait for your best" or something. I mean that you needed this to happen in order to drag out all those horrible feelings and confront the truth about yourself. You needed to be exposed.

I don't mean to diminish what you're going through and I know it hurts, more than you could know. But the fact that you became "overwhelmed with anger, sorrow, self-pity, and jealousy" already shows you're not ready for this relationship right now.

This is a hard thing for me to say and I'm sure you want to fight it. If I do sound insensitive right now, you can stop reading at this very word, and I'll understand.

But let's say you ended up with this guy and got everything you ever wanted. In your current state, you might have been overly controlling and paranoid and envious and then suffocated him. The relationship would've been idolized right at the start, and it would've shrank you into a person you never wanted to be.

Again, maybe I'm presuming too much. I could be way off. But you asked, "How do I move forward and learn to find my identity and security in God alone?" Well this is it, my sister. This is the way. This is your time now to find security in Him.

When James says, *Consider it pure joy whenever you face trials of many kinds, for the testing of your faith develops perseverance* — this is not some cute bumper sticker verse for inspiration. The *testing of your faith* means that [when hard stuff happens, your true essence will be revealed.] All the nasty stuff comes flying out of the basement. It's not pretty. You're finding out what you've grounded your faith in, *what you're really about.* Say hello to the ugliness inside, and say hello to God coming at you with the force of a five-thousand ton freight train to confront you in all His grace and discipline.

But James also concludes: *Let perseverance finish its work so that you may be mature and complete, not lacking anything.* This is good news. It means that when all your craziness is revealed, **both you and God can get to work on that, so that you'd be mature and complete, not lacking anything for the next season of your life**. It means you can sculpt and chisel and cut away at the messy junk of your soul until you are made whole in Him. Whatever ejected from your system: God aims to mold it into a brand new person.

It's so that when an even better guy comes along, you'd actually be ready. Sure, you might still have meltdowns and freak-outs because that's part of being human, but it won't disorient you — because you've been through the valley with God on that one.

Here's what I'm not saying. I don't think every instance of loss is some kind of lesson from God. I don't think it's punishment. We can't spiritualize our pain. It doesn't always wrap up in a bowtie. And I'm not saying you did anything wrong, at all. It's not my place to say those things. But I do think **it's our choice to let go of a possibly**

**false dream and replace it with a total submission to God —
because He knows the dream we ought to have before we have
it.**

Our dreams are not always good ones, and when they come true,
they can become nightmares. I would know. And I don't want you
to be the type of lady that stalks your former crush, or tries to
complicate things with him now, or tries to retain a death-grip on
what you thought you "earned," or squeezes life from your next
relationship. As much as you're torn up over this, please don't let it
make you worse. Let the testing of your faith build into Christ for
continued perseverance and maturity, so that piece by piece, you will
lack nothing.

My dear friend, I know this outcome isn't what you had so
longingly hoped for. We don't always get what we want in life. But
now it is time to find yourself in Christ, to grab His calling, to regain
grounding, to recompose in His rest. Go have fun with your lady-
friends, grab a hamburger and some ice cream, pray your tears and
fears, and sing loud on Sunday. God has an endless love and grace
for you in this very moment, and He sent His Son to die for the very
hurt you're going through. Allow that to motivate you forward, and
you will yet find another dream.

*"Part of my problem was that I was treating my situation like it was a
problem to solve. It's wasn't. It was a season of my life that God had appointed
for me. ... God doesn't do busy work. He doesn't torment us for his own
amusement. He doesn't waste time.*

*"If you're in a tough season of life, there's a purpose to it. Rather than
escaping, work on placing your focus completely on God. Worship him despite
your frustration. And reject any thought which doesn't say God is for you, not
against you."[46]*

— Thomas Christianson

[46] http://thomaschristianson.tumblr.com/post/10199813506/when-god-doesnt-give-
you-what-you-want

## 4. But I Already Crossed A Sexual Boundary: Am I Doomed Forever?[47]

"Recently I got involved with a girl that I really liked for a long time. Unfortunately, things are moving a little faster than I would like and it's largely my fault. Today, we even did sexual acts, though we did not go all the way. I am wondering if it is possible to return this relationship to a place where it is glorifying to God. I also feel like crappy because of guilt and regret. How do I deal with the sexual sin? Is it sexual sin if you did not go all the way?"

My dear wonderful friend: Thank you for your honesty here and sharing such a personal story. Again, I don't feel entirely qualified to speak on this because I've had my share of failures in the past, but please allow me to be a lighthouse for you so that you would not crash your boat as I did.

*what a good analogy*

**The good news is that it's *never too late* to return a relationship back to centering on God.** If you know about David and Bathsheba, then you'll know that despite David's horrible sin — sleeping with a married woman and then killing her husband — they decided to stay together and had a boy named Solomon, the wisest man in all of human history.

I'm not at all condoning what David did. He did suffer some wrenching consequences. But any decision that has a bad start can be reversed toward the glory of God. If God's grace can cover David, then certainly God's got your back too. While your guilt is a natural response, please don't let it crush you into further self-loathing.

The tough news is that by falling to temptation —

---

[47] This is also in my book *What The Church Won't Talk About,* available on Amazon.
I've updated this post as well.

1) You have increased your appetite for sin, and

2) You have weakened your resolve to fight against it.

This doesn't mean that the relationship has to be over. It only means that you'll need a more wisdom-filled **Battle Plan** to deal with the issue. You'll be tempted now to keep going physical, and this will prevent you from really getting to know her for *her*.

This means you'll need accountability with mature Christians. It means *no ninja-dating* — it's unwise to sneak around behind her parents' back or without counseling from your pastor. It means having wisdom about your time, your space, your triggers. In a sense, it will mean fasting from certain physical contact until you're both married.

The best way to know these boundaries is simply hang out with your lady as if she were a male friend. I wish I had a much more profound method here, but that's the simplest rule to follow.

If you absolutely feel like you can't do this: then break up. Wait until you're ready. I'm not trying to be a moralistic old-fashioned preacher here, but I'm saying this to promote your maximum joy. I meet too many couples who think they can handle each other, but they end up in miserable exhausting cycles of defeat because they weren't willing to be wise and disciplined. I don't think breaking up is always a first option, but it's not a last resort either.

If you decide to keep pursuing this, remember that if you only set physical boundaries to run from sin, you'll always fail. You need to run toward something too. The battle against lust can't be just about running from sin, but also about running to God's purposes, plans, His presence, and His people.

There are no magic words to turn off lust. There's nothing I could say that would make you want purity without turning you into a self-whipping flagellator. The only way to beat this is to *circumvent your desires towards a greater desire, so that you are funneling your energy into the perfect will of Christ.* It's a messy process, for sure, but it's one you can start today.

Please keep in mind: the small victories are worth celebrating.

When you're about to mess up,

when you're in that space where it feels like there's no return,

when the lights are off and you're both alone and it feels like it's a done deal,

or you're down the spiral of that website again—

*It's not too late.* **You can still choose.**

*You can grab your clothes and run like hell.*

*You can close your laptop, shut it all off, and flee for your life.*

And while this isn't some perfect victory, that's okay. You still fought the gravitational pull of a bad choice. I'm cheering for you here, and so is Jesus.


Consider serving together with your girlfriend in some kind of ministry opportunity. Whether it's feeding the homeless or babysitting for families or starting a project to raise funds for orphans or leading a Bible Study or building houses downtown, go discover what God has specifically wired both of you for and then pursue His heart for the world.

As Francis Chan said, all couples are two people with one mission, and following God together will already solve most of your problems.[48] This is definitely not easy and it won't be a perfect journey. But the decision to pursue this relationship and the motivation to keep it going is knowing that this is about getting on God's adventure together with your one life on this earth, to know that nothing is more exciting for a couple than to take God's hand and set sail for His unfolding story.

You will then barely even have to fight lust because you won't need to. Of course it will still be tough, but now you're both fighting

---

[48] "Two People With One Mission,"
https://www.youtube.com/watch?v=ruPVtcXD2Kw

*towards* something greater than yourselves. You will have a motivation simply beyond being "good" or "pure." You might even find out while dating that you're both not meant for each other, but you won't be breaking up because of lust. It will instead be about finding a partner to serve Him.

My friend, I know this sounds like pretty words on a page. It sounds theoretical. None of this is meant to be an instant cure. It will require a daily conscious choice from you to have a God-centered relationship, to repent of lesser things, to be a leader, to protect the sacredness of a woman's dignity. It requires your entire reliance on God in a way that you might never have before. In short, you will become a man. I hope you consider the seriousness of this task, and at the same time enjoy this relationship by serving our God together. I pray you will both cling to Him for not only His wisdom and strength, but also His purposes.

## 5. About To Marry A Porn Addict

"Hi! I enjoy reading your blog and I know you have battled a porn addiction. I have a few questions. How do you feel about people who are battling against a porn addiction while dating? Do you think that person could have a genuinely Christ-centered, Godly and healthy relationship? Or is it bound to fail? Would it be okay for the guy to take a break so he figures things out for himself? What is the role of the girl in this? Is she able to do anything at all?"

"I'm engaged to someone who claims to be Christian but I'm starting to feel as though he is not. We agree on almost everything except for the issue on whether watching porn is okay ... He just wants me to be okay with it, that way he doesn't feel guilty. So my question is, is watching porn wrong? ...What biblical evidence is there that I can give him? I really pray that he would want to change but if not I don't think I can marry someone with this problem."

If you would've asked me this question a few years ago, I would've said:

*"What are you thinking, ladies? Dump that dude right now! Any man who can't give up something for you ain't no man at all."*

To some degree, I still agree with this. If it's not serious or you just started dating, then please don't feel obligated to stay. You deserve better. If you're looking for an excuse to stay with this guy because he's cute in the face or you're afraid to be alone, then you already know that won't be enough down the line.

But in my growing compassion for people, I know how difficult it is to defeat porn in an over-sexualized culture. I know how messed up we are to think that "porn is the norm." As much as I sound like a cranky old man, sex has become like shaking hands and human trafficking is barely blinked at. This is our world now: a culture of deep apathy that is unavoidably ingrained.

While this doesn't absolve *any* man's destructive behavior, it does give me more of a heart to work with them and resolve the root issues. It helps explain why men shrug it off.

Maybe you've been told to dump the guy on the spot, and that could be good advice — but battling porn is a lifelong war for *all* men (and women) today. It's unrealistic to think you'll meet some guy who has never struggled with it.

I also know how hard it is to just break up with someone if you're engaged or it's very serious. Certainly we should never be afraid to break off a relationship that is abusive or a deadbeat, but porn is something you both could overcome together with patience and persistence. It's not always a deal-breaker.

While you might find the perfect porn-less guy, I think we can realistically say that every woman will now have to openly, honestly, aggressively talk about lust with their future husbands in an era where porn is so freely available (and husbands, with wives too). This has to be a daily truthful dialogue where the man must be able to freely express himself without shame or a fear of retaliation.

But first, let's talk about what will happen if the guy says, "I just want you to be okay with my porn." This will sound like I'm guilt-tripping, but I want both men and women to know how serious this gets.

1) If you're planning on marrying this guy one day, you will probably have kids. Your future husband will be awkward around your daughter when she turns thirteen *because porn has turned his view of women into objectification.* He'll also be awkward around your daughter's friends.

Out of guilt, he'll try to avoid your daughter or will be plain uncomfortable — and she'll feel alienated, rejected, and lacking in a father's love, sending her down a spiral of seeking fulfillment and acting out. You might think this is crazy talk, but I've heard of this happening *way* too much.

2) Even if you both have a son, then your husband will be awkward around your son's future girlfriend. That's not going anywhere good.

3) Porn has a way of destroying self-control that bleeds into other areas, like finances, health, cheating, lying, and being able to spend sacrificial time with other people.

4) However society feels about porn and however much they accept it, if a guy is not willing to give that up for you, that already says a ton about who he is. Also, secular circles are catching up and now realizing[49] how harmful it really is.[50] The research is showing that long-term use of porn leads to erectile dysfunction, even in teens. I would laugh if it wasn't so sad.

5) Much of the porn industry is directly related to human trafficking and sex slavery.[51] It's *not* from women who are willing, as they're so often portrayed. So using porn (even "free porn") is directly supporting a horrific multi-million dollar industry of rape, torture, abuse, and under-aged coercion. This is one of the main reasons I decided to quit porn. I couldn't live with myself knowing I was endorsing the institutionalized rape of young women. Reading some of the stories nearly made me vomit.

*watch this*

---

[49] http://www.huffingtonpost.com/lauren-dubinsky/porn-addiction_b_1686481.html
[50] Gary Wilson, "The Great Porn Experiment." At TEDxGlasgow. http://youtu.be/wSF82AwSDiU
[51] My personal research showed high correlations between sex trafficking victims, prostitutions, sex offenders who use pornography (nearly 100%), those who video-recorded sex trafficked victims, and psychological coercion to entice women (and men) into the porn industry. While not all pornography qualifies as the solid definition of human trafficking, there is an undeniable link of causation and overlap between many of these issues.

Now all that to say: I don't think a relationship with a porn-using guy is necessarily bound to fail, but you *absolutely* must have a heart-to-heart eye-to-eye discussion with him. You'll really need to dig at the root of his motives, to see if he is willing to be honest with himself, and see if he really cares to change. The evidence is undeniable. [If he can't quit, he can't be the kind of husband or father that's worthy of you.]

You're potentially entrusting this person to take care of business, to be faithful, be stable, be constant, be a leader, and to take care of your children that will pop out of you — and you are sharing your life with him until the day you die. Women: *it's a very scary thing to marry a man and to entrust him with such a lifetime commitment.* It's even harder if you're beginning from a deficit of stubborn refusal.

*dang, that's crazy*

So ask the hard questions. Why won't he give up the porn? What advantages are there to it? Does he really need a magical Bible verse to stop him? If the Bible never said a word on it, would porn ever honor God? Is it okay to support an industry that enslaves young women? Can't he give this up *for you*?

This might take many conversations. You can refer him to counseling or to seek a men's group or to check out the research. I hope he is open to this. I hope he comes around to the truth. But if he completely refuses to quit or doesn't try at all: then you're going to have to consider a tough decision.

I'll definitely throw you a prayer. My heart is with you, dear friends. When it comes down to it, please be willing to put your foot down and to *never* settle for less. There are still godly men out there who are definitely not perfect, but more than willing to move the moon for you.

## 6. I've Totally Screwed Up And I Can't Pick Up The Pieces

"Hi J.S. Park, I'm a recovering sex addict and porn viewer. I'm a female. I gave my life to Jesus and started in a 6 year relationship with a brother from church that resulted into engagement. In a state of emotional uncertainty and mental vulnerability, I allowed one of his groomsmen to emotionally/sexually prey on me; I consented. I entered into a sexual relationship for 7 months and just got out of it. What's worse, with this other fellow, we taught Sunday school, he's my brother's spiritual mentor and leads a small group. We stopped this sin and he has since not spoken to me out of anger, but he continues to continue to invest himself and is not remorseful. I've come out to others but I know I have created a wave of destruction in my church. The shame and guilt are eating at me. What should I do? Please help."

My dear beloved friend, I have to first say that I'm angry with you here at these men who chose to take advantage of you and did not own up to their actions, and while God still has grace for them, grace also means truth and correction. I know you said you consented, but it doesn't make what they did any less wrong.

Unfortunately, there will be some choices we make that have irreversible consequences, and it will feel impossible to move forward. You'll try so hard to pick up the pieces and go back to how it used to be, but I think you're learning this might never happen.

Many of us respond in different ways to shattered situations, such as:

- Binge-eating, binge-drinking, binge-shopping, binge-sex, binge-everything.

- Packing up and changing cities.

- Leaving the church for good.

- Depression, isolation, constant regret, and suicidal behavior.

- Emotional paralysis, shut-down, and antisocial tendencies.
- Aggression, violence, bitterness, and resentment — especially at God.
- Choosing to do whatever you want to do, because you feel you're now "damaged goods."

I know things are really screwed up and you'll be tempted to do any of the above, but my dear friend, *none of these things have to be your story*. I completely understand the trapped feeling of being among others who constantly remind you of what happened, but even if things fall apart, it doesn't mean *you* have to. In the worst of times, you can still choose to do the best you can, however imperfectly.

Maybe you've heard this before, but really, you can only get bitter or better. You are heading for a **breakdown** or **breakthrough**. It's really okay to feel you're not okay, but I don't think it's okay to stay there.[52] It's awesome that you're honest and you're allowed to feel what you feel, but let that push you towards growth instead of regression.

In fact, your situation is *more* reason to grow, and not less.

I don't mean to package your hurt into an afterschool special with a moral at the end. Yet at the end, we still make a choice in how we move forward. Nothing about you is over yet.

In case you think this is just pretty pep talk, I've really heard it all. I've spoken with people that have similar stories:

- My friend cheated on his wife with a married woman, and they all have kids. One of them is a Sunday school teacher.
- Another friend has been raped by at least two guys in the area, and they all still hang out like nothing happened. They all attend church.
- Another friend was sexually molested as a child by a pastor who leads a church in town.

---

[52] Inspired by Matt Chandler, lead pastor of the Village Church in Texas.

- A youth pastor was recently discovered to have slept with almost every female teenager in his youth group.

- In my early days before I was a pastor, I slept with one of the members of the praise team. I say this to my own deep shame and horror.

In nearly all these situations, I've been able to see how the events unfolded. And for the most part, *many of them chose to continue messing it up, even after they were forgiven and shown grace.*

In this very moment, even if your entire church were to embrace you again, you still have your story ahead of you. You still decide who you're going to be from here on out. And amidst the broken pieces, you can still be whole.

I don't have the silver bullet to fix up your specific circumstance. I can only encourage you to be patient, be humble, be loving, and don't look back. You don't need to do that perfectly, either. People will judge you regardless, because they're people. Please don't let that change you for the worse. I would hope that your church realizes you don't need more guilt than you're already feeling and that the consequences themselves are enough. Even if not, you don't have to constantly hang your head in church. Don't worry about compensating to "win back" friendships. Once you've apologized, you don't need to keep apologizing. Don't be pressured into a guilt-driven humility.

And you don't have to protect anyone like this. Tell the leaders about who is preying on others so they can enforce discipline. It's not cool that you were victimized, but you're also not a victim. If you were leading this church, you'd certainly want to know if this was happening. Tell the right people and don't be afraid to take action for justice.

I must also add: *God absolutely loves you* and He's *crazy about you no matter what*. In our rock-bottom moments of ill

God Absolutely loves you!

consequences, it's easy to think that God's response towards us is disappointment or frustration. But God sent His Son exactly for this very reason — to draw you near Him in spite of yourself. Don't ever let self-pity get in the way of this; don't ever feel you have to pay off your guilt with self-inflicted punishment. God did the work for you already. He preempted your failures and saw your sin coming a mile away, but He loved you anyway. He will not time-warp His Son off the cross. He says in Jeremiah 31:3, *"I have loved you with an everlasting love."*

I know it feels like you're walking in a fog you created. and there will be some tough days ahead, but God is with you in this to the very end. **Pace yourself and don't rush the healing process and please have grace for you, too**. If you mess it up again, get back up. God is there to cheer you on and restore you for next time. There's no such thing as "too late" with God. When your church or your family or the whole world will not give you a second chance, God is the God of infinite chances. His grace is that big. Continue to stumble after Him.

Please don't let the weight of your consequences say anything less about you as a person, because God continually has grace for you in the middle of the mess.

### 7. Six Ways To Be Ready To Pursue A Relationship

**"Hey brother, hope all has been well. Just wanted to throw a question at you. I've always wondered about the specific things that a man should do when he has feelings for a sister in Christ. I'm not really talking about the tangible things, like how to talk to her, but more-so what he should do internally, on himself. Examples, what should he pray for, what should he be cautious with? Stuff like that. Hope all is well, God bless."**

I want to be careful here that I don't turn all this into a magic formula, but I'm also certain you'll consider this with deliberate care and thoughtful prayer. As always, please feel free to skip around.

#### 1) Be okay with rejection.

If this lady doesn't know your feelings yet, then I hope it's cool if you just stay friends. Once again, *there's no such thing as a friend-zone*. You're either two human beings, or you're two human beings who happen to be dating. I don't mean that you'll be all chipper about it — of course it hurts to be rejected — but you won't flip a table or sob about it for half a year. That would convey a deeper fundamental problem of control issues or obsessive attachment.

#### 2) Be prepared to confront yourself.

I think most advice on dating covers the initial phase of dating. That's probably the first three months, which is equivalent to learning Twinkle Little Star on the piano. But after the blinding honeymoon phase is over, you're going to find that *you're way more selfish than you ever dared imagine*. It's a shocking rude awakening, and even after dating for nearly five years, I still find terrible selfish desires in my dirty messed-up heart.

It's really not your fault. It's just how we are. For all our dramatic pop-radio songs about "love is sacrifice," no one's naturally good at this. It's really hard to prioritize your life with someone, and when all the cuteness is over, it'll feel like you're killing a part of yourself to share life with her. Be prepared to confront all the ugliness of your selfish soul. I've known people who get married in their thirties, and they found it *dang near impossible* to give up their single-life habits. Think of your money, your time, your spirituality, your family, all the things you hold sacred, and you're going to let another person into your territory with the raw power of a freight train.

Simply expect that you'll be selfish and that *she is not the enemy,* and that will be half the battle.

My life verse (and the idea behind my blog and podcast) has been Psalm 139:23-24. It's the second passage I ever memorized (the first was Colossians 3:2). David writes:

*Search me, O God, and know my heart; test me and know my anxious thoughts. See if there is any offensive way in me, and lead me in the way everlasting.*

I pray through this continually. It has been the most important personal Bible passage for my growth. I pray it blesses you too.

### 3) Pray for continually strong friendships.

You'll need a strong base of male friends (or female if you're female) to keep you *you.* I've seen dudes run into the nether void when they get a girlfriend and break off all meaningful contact with their friends. They begin to set all their dials with their girlfriend, making the guy lose a part of himself down the line. This probably sounds silly or sexist right now, but please believe me: *your girlfriend cannot be everything you need her to be.* She can't replace your same-gender friends, or else you'll end up demanding all the wrong intimacy from her. And if you think, "I'll never be the guy that loses touch with his boys!" — you might be the guy most likely to do that.

Not all friends stay friends forever, because our lives and seasons change. So pray that for each season, you have a strong community of friends who can both have fun *and* be willing to gently rebuke you. And pray for a heart of humility that can hear the hard truth about yourself.

### 4) Seek a lot of wisdom and pastoral counsel.

It helped me a lot to hang out with old couples and married pastors just to *observe* what they were like together. I wanted to see what was good and not good. I asked tons of annoying questions. I asked how they fought lust before marriage, how they melded personalities, how they argued things out, how they raised their kids. I asked how God worked in their relationship. We sometimes have a way of shunning older married people as "old-fashioned" or out-of-touch, but our elders are incredible fountains of wisdom that *want* to share what they know. I've really been blessed by being nosy about their business, and they were always willing to pass on their knowledge.

### 5) Be ready to lead with confidence.

You're mostly going to be the spiritual tempo-setter in your relationship. Whatever you think about Ephesians 5:21-33, I know one thing: *I've never met a woman who doesn't want a guy that can lead.* No woman willingly says, "Yeah, it's fine if he sucks at leading. I guess the kids that pop out of my womb can fend for themselves while my husband sits on the couch watching Doctor Who all day."

Once a dude asked me, "But what if my girlfriend is spiritually more mature than me? Why can't she lead?" After I stopped punching him in the groin, I told him, "Are you okay with your future daughter dating a guy who's like that? Don't you think what you just said is *more reason* to step it up and not less? Can't you wake up, America?"

Confidence is not bravado or macho-manliness. I don't mean that you won't make mistakes or that you'll be a perfect leader. I mean: Use this time wisely to pursue all the truth and wisdom and grace of God, so that you enter the fray with fruits blooming. Your confidence comes from a complete dependent reliance on God, from whom you'll be drawing all possible strength. Anything else can't give you the rock-solid foundation of confidence you'll need for both dating and marriage.

I have to add here that *you cannot go faster than the woman wants to.* If you go too fast, you'll end up coercing her into things she'll only do to make you happy, and she will regret every second of it. Once you cross certain boundaries, it's hard to go back. I've made my share of mistakes here too, so keep it slow and steady.

### 6) Pursue Christ and you'll be just fine.

When we have a crush on someone, there's a tendency to center our lives around them. We make every song on the radio about this girl; we brush our teeth harder, use a bit more hair gel, and even change our boxers every day. I'm not saying this is wrong. I'm saying: Please don't let your heart stray into this sort of flex-to-impress mentality. Your life is not about finding that special someone. It has always been and always will be about living for the glory of God by the grace of God through the love of God. Anything less is settling for less.

Regardless of how your dating life goes, the Gospel is still the most important thing about you. Once you're dating, the Gospel will continue to inform how you treat your lady, how you raise children, how you handle finances, how you confront the ugliness in your own heart — not to mention your eternity. You already know that, but dating and relationships have a way of squashing us into myopic complacency. We too easily forget about God's mission and leave behind all that risk-taking, cross-bearing, self-denying passion.

Apostle Paul admonishes both married couples and singles to remember the urgency of our mission in 1 Corinthians 7, saying —

*"For this world in its present form is passing away ... An unmarried man is concerned about the Lord's affairs—how he can please the Lord. But a married man is concerned about the affairs of this world ... I am saying this for*

*your own good, not to restrict you, but that you may live in a right way in undivided devotion to the Lord."*

I've seen a funny thing happen when men or women forget about their crushes and simply pursue God. Along the way, *they find someone else who is passionately pursuing Christ too.* I love it when this happens. If you're on the adventure that Christ has designed you for, then "Christian dating" is merely inviting someone to merge their adventure with you. It's fun, it's electric, and it's glorious. So pursue God — and maybe you'll find others in pursuit.

# Chapter 5
# Starting Over Means Finishing Strong

We met at church. When we began dating, we were as slow as snails. In the first few months, we decided to have a forty day fast from each other to pray about the whole thing, because we wanted to be ready for what we were getting into. We weren't supposed to see each other but we broke the fast about seven times. We also wrote in our own journals for the forty days, and I gave her mine. She kept hers, and of course, I absolutely wanted to respect her privacy. She still laughs at all the pictures I drew in my journal; she was a penguin, and I was a gorilla.

I remember on one of our first dates, it was raining and I carried her on my back across a dock with no railings. We ran all the way out and back. One wrong move and we both would've fell in the water and that would've ruined the whole thing, but she held on and I didn't let go. She screamed and laughed. I wish I could've seen her face. Thank God I didn't have a stroke.

When she would get sick, I would bring a cold ginger ale and various foods and wait around until she felt better. Whenever I got sick she came by with food and made sure I didn't die. She asked me what kind of food I wanted and I told her to surprise me. She always got what I wanted. I started looking forward to illness.

We saw Hilllsong together, and *Wicked,* and watched the manatees at Homosassa Springs do barrel rolls. We read the Bible over the phone and prayed for each other.

But she saw flashes of the darkness I tried to hide. At the three year mark, I scared her. She ended it, and I understood. At some point I had become completely unapproachable.

-

After the break-up, I went through about a billion things. I had a nervous breakdown. I took a two month break from ministry. I was clinically depressed. I hated myself, and nearly every morning, I cussed out my reflection in the mirror. But I also fought, hard. I quit my old habits, got in touch with God again, and learned to love and forgive through all that was happening. And I adopted a dog named Rosco.

Even though it was painful: the six month break-up was the best thing my fiancé could've ever done for me.

I needed those six months.

I needed to clear my head and to get right with God.

It was as simple as that.

During the six months, I was finally able to confess my fifteen year porn addiction, and *quit*. I've been sober over three years now. When I say sober, I don't mean that I haven't ever looked at porn again. About a dozen times in those three years, I started on the familiar trail of websites, but each time, *I was able to shut it down and stop*. My pants stayed on. I was able to snap out of it and flee back to Christ.

I had an anger problem. I sought counseling; I paid therapists; I found a pastor of a large church who was willing to open up his office for me, over and over, just to talk. He once told me, *"You have a Public Self, a Private Self, and then the You that God wants you to be. And right now, you're not you. Don't you know that if Jesus were walking the earth right now, he would actually look for you and pick even a guy like you? We can't understand how huge that is."*

I read the book of Galatians almost every day. I called people who used to be friends and I apologized for every outburst, every hurtful word, without a single excuse. I wrote in a journal by hand, just wrote and wrote until the edges frayed to the spiral. I visited fourteen different churches during my two month sabbatical, and sometimes, God even showed up.

I was done beating myself up with self-hate.

I was done bowing to my old self.

[I started over with the Most High, who met me at my most low.]

That's how it often goes.

-

Six months later, during my two month sabbatical, Julette and I happened to meet again. We were both near a Starbucks out of town, a coincidence (or as people say, God's providence in disguise). I told her I still loved her, and I wanted to make it work, and I wouldn't give up. She thought about it, and she could see I was changing, had changed. She agreed. We took it as slow as snails again.

A couple years later, I proposed to her on the beach at night on a portable table with a chocolate cheesecake and tiny Christmas lights.

I told her, "I've done a lot of wrong things in my life. But going after you was not one of them."

"I'm so glad you did," she said. And on Valentine's Day, the corniest day of the year, we were engaged.

-

I don't want you to think that every story has this sort of ending. It doesn't. I've failed and fallen so many more times in between.

I've sat down with enough singles and couples and broken-up people to know that many stories end in permanent loss. The only reason I might know half of what I do is because I've simply listened to story after story of tragedy, cheating, and trauma. I've seen and heard the worst of people. At times I would get two completely different versions of how it went down, but it's all the same: we live in a world of dead dreams that stay dead and buried.

Yet if there's any real formula I could impart to you, it's simple.

In the midst of our disintegrating surroundings, no one knows how the story will end. Abraham didn't. Joseph didn't. Naomi and Ruth didn't. Esther didn't. David didn't. Peter and Paul and Mary didn't. Some of them never resolved their tension; they went to the grave with unfinished conflicts and unfulfilled hopes.

I didn't know that I would be engaged to the woman who rightly called it quits on me.

**Yet I had to keep going anyway.** And even if my momentum forward wouldn't "win" her back, I had to be okay with that too. *In letting go of my own dream, I was able to become the person that God had always dreamed I could be.*

This is how we finish strong, by starting over with the originator of such strength, by the one who writes the better conclusion.

When we don't know where we'll end, we can still choose who we'll be when we get there.

You might have heard something like that before, but an old truth is no less true or wonderful. It's old because it's timeless, and it works.

Even if I hadn't ended up with my fiancé now, even if David had missed Goliath, even if Shadrach, Meshach, and Abednego had blown up, even if Daniel had been lion food — we would've been okay. We would've went out, on our own terms, in the arms of God.

We could end this thing by grace.

I'm making this sound much prettier than it really is, but this process of becoming a God-shaped person will take you to places you don't want to go, into the valley of the shadow of death, into Nero's garden on a pyre, into dangerous nations and fatherless prisons and long seasons of friendless silence, and most especially into the contours of your own ugly heart.

But there, dear friend, is where our molecules are violently re-engineered, to live.

It's there that you are finally free to fail, to lose, to sacrifice pride and anger and hate.

It's there that you become ready to be single, to be married, to be persecuted, to be demoted, to lead, to fight an army, to fight yourself.

It's there you no longer need to impress others or win validation or manipulate your environment or build your portfolio or beat the other guy.

It's there that even death is healed.

I can't say I'm fully there yet; we're still on our way.

But I hope to see you there, my friend. By grace, to the horizon, together.7

—J.S.

By grace
to the
HORIZON

together.

# Acknowledged

A shout-out of gratitude to the dozens of test-readers who spotted errors, made fair criticisms, offered prayers, and invested their time to fully engage. It's a lot to commit to reading a whole book, and I never want to take for granted your effort and your wisdom.

A big thank you to Lauren Britt of yesdarlingido.tumblr, who has so far test-read both my books and wrote the wonderful Foreword. I'm honored and I'm a fan for life.

Another big thank you to T.B. LaBerge, my wonderful brother in Christ on Tumblr, as we silently reblog each other's posts and encourage one another. You have a kind heart and I aspire to write as well as you do.

A shout-out to pastors Timothy Keller, Andy Stanley, and Francis Chan. You each shaped how I see Jesus, and your material on dating reminded me there are bigger things than dating.

A shout-out to Joshua Harris. I dig you, brother. Even if some of the criticism might be fair, nobody has to agree to love each other, and I hope the church (and me) gets this right first.

I must again thank my first pastor, Pastor Paul Kim, who endured with me as I went through many bad relationships for years, and he never judged me once. I'm sure it was a stressful time to be my pastor then, but you showed such grace it melted me. I wouldn't be the person I am today without your Christ-saturated heart.

Of course, to my beautiful fiancé. I can't believe I get to marry you. You were there when I was jobless, penniless, lost, at my end, at my best and worst, during cry-face and baby voice and when I spent hours staring at a screen to write a single word. You were there for my first terrible sermon as a new seminarian and eventually there for that crowded room when you saw the man I had become. I could only hope I was there for you as much as I wanted to be. I'm excited for our future. I love you, and don't ever forget it.

38757135R00093

Made in the USA
Lexington, KY
23 January 2015